The Whale Rider

Witi Ihimaera was born in Gisbourne, New Zealand in 1944. (The Mauri name for New Zealand is Aotearoa.) He was the first Maori writer to publish both a book of short stories, *Pounamu Pounamu* (1972), and a novel *Tangi* (1973).

Witi was interested in writing from an early age, and saw writing as a valuable opportunity to express in print his experience of being a Maori.

The Whale Rider is a magical, mythical work about a young girl whose relationship with a whale ensures the salvation of her village. It is, says Witi, the work of his 'that the Maori community accepts best'.

THE
WHALE RIDER

WITI IHIMAERA

Heinemann

Inspiring generations

Heinemann is an imprint of Pearson Education Limited,
a company incorporated in England and Wales, having
its registered office at Edinburgh Gate, Harlow, Essex, CM20 2JE.
Registered company number: 872828

Heinemann is a registered trademark of Pearson Education Limited

First published in Great Britain in 2005 by Harcourt Education Ltd
First published in the New Windmills Series 2005

14

British Library Cataloguing in Publication Data is available
from the British Library on request.

ISBN 978 0 435131 08 1

Cover design by GD Associates
Typeset by ⋌ Tek-Art, Croydon, Surrey

Printed in China (CTPS/14)

For Jessica Kiri and Olivia Ata,
The best girls in the whole wide world

This story is set in Whangara, on the East Coast of New Zealand, where Paikea is the tipuna ancestor. However, the story, people and events described are entirely fictional and have not been based on any people in Whangara.

He tohu aroha ki a Whangara me nga uri o Paikea.

Thanks also to Julia Keelan, Caroline Haapu and Hekia Parata for their advice and assistance.

May the calm be widespread
May the ocean glisten as greenstone
May the shimmer of light
Ever dance across your pathway

Contents

Prologue

The Whale Rider

One

In the old days, in the years that have gone before us, the land and sea felt a great emptiness, a yearning. The mountains were like a stairway to heaven, and the lush green rainforest was a rippling cloak of many colours. The sky was iridescent, swirling with the patterns of wind and clouds; sometimes it reflected the prisms of rainbow or southern aurora. The sea was ever-changing, shimmering and seamless to the sky. This was the well at the bottom of the world and when you looked into it you felt you could see to the end of forever.

This is not to say that the land and sea were without life, without vivacity. The tuatara, the ancient lizard with its third eye, was sentinel here, unblinking in the hot sun, watching and waiting to the east. The moa browsed in giant wingless herds across the southern island. Within the warm stomach of the rainforests, kiwi, weka and the other birds foraged for huhu and similar succulent insects. The forests were loud with the clatter of tree bark, chatter of cicada and murmur of fish-laden streams. Sometimes the forest grew suddenly quiet and in wet bush could be heard the filigree of fairy laughter like a sparkling glissando.

The sea, too, teemed with fish but they also seemed to be waiting. They swam in brilliant shoals, like rains of glittering dust, throughout the greenstone depths – hapuku, manga, kahawai, tamure, moki and warehou – herded by shark or mango ururoa. Sometimes from far off a white shape would be seen flying through the sea but it would only be the serene flight of the tarawhai, the stingray with the spike on its tail.

Waiting. Waiting for the seeding. Waiting for the gifting. Waiting for the blessing to come.

Suddenly, looking up at the surface, the fish began to see the dark bellies of the canoes from the east. The first of the Ancients were coming, journeying from their island kingdom beyond the horizon. Then, after a period, canoes were seen to be returning to the east, making long cracks on the surface sheen. The land and the sea sighed with gladness:

We have been found.
The news is being taken back to the place of the Ancients.
Our blessing will come soon.

In that waiting time, earth and sea began to feel the sharp pangs of need, for an end to the yearning. The forests sent sweet perfumes upon the eastern winds and garlands of pohutukawa upon the eastern tides. The sea flashed continuously with flying fish leaping high to look beyond the horizon and to be the first to announce the coming; in the shallows, the chameleon seahorses pranced at attention. The only reluctant ones were the fairy people who retreated with their silver laughter to caves in glistening waterfalls.

The sun rose and set, rose and set. Then one day, at its noon apex, the first sighting was made. A spume on the horizon. A dark shape rising from the greenstone depths of the ocean, awesome, leviathan, breaching through the surface and hurling itself skyward before falling seaward again. Underwater the muted thunder boomed like a great door opening far away, and both sea and land trembled from the impact of that downward plunging.

Suddenly the sea was filled with awesome singing, a song with eternity in it, a song to the land:

You have called and I have come,
bearing the gift of the Gods

The dark shape rising, rising again. A whale, gigantic. A sea monster. Just as it burst through the sea, a flying fish leaping high in its ecstasy saw water and air streaming like thunderous foam from that noble beast and knew, ah yes, that the time had come. For the sacred sign was on the monster, a swirling tattoo imprinted on the forehead.

Then the flying fish saw that astride the head, as it broke skyward, was a man. He was wondrous to look upon, the whale rider. The water streamed away from him and he opened his mouth to gasp in the cold air. His eyes were shining with splendour. His body dazzled with diamond spray. Upon that beast he looked like a small tattooed figurine, dark brown, glistening and erect. He seemed, with all his strength, to be pulling the whale into the sky.

Rising, rising. And the man felt the power of the whale as it propelled itself from the sea. He saw far off the land long sought and now found, and he began to fling small spears seaward and landward on his magnificent journey toward the land.

Some of the spears in mid-flight turned into pigeons which flew into the forests. Others on landing in the sea changed into eels. And the song in the sea drenched the air with ageless music and land and sea opened themselves to him, the gift long waited for: tangata, man. With great gladness and thanksgiving the man cried out to the land.

Karanga mai, karanga mai, karanga mai.

Call me. But there was one spear, so it is told, the last, which, when the whale rider tried to throw it, refused to leave his hand. Try as he might, the spear would not fly.

So the whale rider uttered a prayer over the wooden spear, saying, 'Let this spear be planted in the years to come, for there are sufficient spear already implanted. Let this be the one to flower when the people are troubled and it is most needed.'

And the spear then leapt from his hands with gladness and soared through the sky. It flew across a thousand years. When it hit the earth it did not change but waited for another hundred and fifty years to pass until it was needed.

The flukes of the whale stroked majestically at the sky.

Hui e, haumi e, *taiki e.*

Let it be done.

Spring

The Force of Destiny

Two

The Valdes Peninsula, Patagonia. Te Whiti Te Ra. The nursery, the cetacean crib. The giant whales had migrated four months earlier from their Antarctic feeding range to mate, calve and rear their young in two large, calm bays. Their leader, the ancient bull whale, together with the elderly female whales, fluted whalesongs of benign magnificence as they watched over the rest of the herd. In that glassy sea known as the Pathway of the Sun, and under the turning splendour of the stars, they waited until the newly born were strong enough for the long voyages ahead.

Watching, the ancient bull whale was swept up in memories of his own birthing. His mother had been savaged by sharks three months later; crying over her in the shallows of Hawaiki, he had been succoured by the golden human who became his master. The human had heard the young whale's distress and had come into the sea, playing a flute. The sound was plangent and sad as he tried to communicate his oneness with the young whale's mourning. Quite without the musician knowing it, the melodic patterns of the flute's phrases imitated the whalesong of comfort. The young whale drew nearer to the human, who cradled him and pressed noses with the orphan in greeting. When the herd travelled onward, the young whale remained and grew under the tutelage of his master.

The bull whale had become handsome and virile, and he had loved his master. In the early days his master would play the flute and the whale would come to the call. Even in his lumbering years of age the whale would remember his adolescence and his master; at such moments he would send long, undulating songs of mourning through the lambent water. The elderly females would swim to him hastily, for they loved him, and gently in the dappled warmth they would minister to him.

In a welter of sonics, the ancient bull whale would communicate his nostalgia. And then, in the echoing water, he would hear his master's flute. Straight away the whale would cease his feeding and try to leap out of the sea, as he used to when he was younger and able to speed toward his master.

As the years had burgeoned the happiness of those days was like a siren call to the ancient bull whale. But his elderly females were fearful; for them, that rhapsody of adolescence, that song of the flute, seemed only to signify that their leader was turning his thoughts to the dangerous islands to the southwest.

Three

I suppose that if this story has a beginning it is with Kahu. After all, it was Kahu who was there at the end, and it was Kahu's intervention which perhaps saved us all. We always knew there would be such a child, but when Kahu was born, well, we were looking the other way, really. We were over at our grandparents' place, me and the boys, having a few drinks and a party, when the phone rang.

'A *girl*', Koro Apirana, our grandfather, said, disgusted. 'I will have nothing to do with her. She has broken the male line of descent in our tribe.' He shoved the telephone at our grandmother, Nani Flowers, saying, 'Here. It's your fault. Your female side was too strong.' Then he pulled on his boots and stomped out of the house.

The phone call was from the eldest grandson, my brother Porourangi, who was living in the South Island. His wife, Rehua, had just given birth to the first great-grandchild of our extended family.

'Hello, dear,' Nani Flowers said into the phone. Nani Flowers was used to Koro Apirana's growly ways, although she threatened to divorce him every second day, and I could tell that it didn't bother her if the baby was a girl or a boy. Her lips were quivering with emotion because she had been waiting for the call from Porourangi all month. Her eyes went sort of cross-eyed, as they always did whenever she was overcome with love. 'What's that? What did you say?'

We began to laugh, me and the boys, and we yelled to Nani, 'Hey! Old lady! You're supposed to put the phone to your ear so you can hear!' Nani disliked telephones; most times she was so shaken to hear a voice come out of little holes in the headpiece that she would hold the phone at arm's length. So I went up to her and put the phone against her head.

Next minute, the tears started rolling down the old lady's face. 'What's that, dear? *Oh*, the poor thing. Oh the *poor* thing. Oh the poor *thing*. Oh. Oh. Oh. Well you tell Rehua that the first is the worst. The others come easier because by then she'll have the hang of it. Yes, dear. I'll tell him. Yes, don't you worry. Yes. All right. Yes, and we love you too.'

She put down the phone. 'Well, Rawiri,' she said to me, 'you and the boys have got a beautiful niece. She must be, because Porourangi said she looks just like me.' We tried not to laugh, because Nani was no film star. Then, all of a sudden, she put her hands on her hips and made her face grim and went to the front verandah. Far away, down on the beach, old Koro Apirana was putting his rowboat onto the afternoon sea. Whenever he felt angry he would always get on his rowboat and row out into the middle of the ocean to sulk.

'*Hey*,' Nani Flowers boomed, 'you old paka,' which was the affectionate name she always called our Koro when she wanted him to know she loved him. 'Hey!' But he pretended he didn't hear her calling him an old bugger, jumped into the rowboat, and made out to sea.

Well, that did it. Nani Flowers got her wild up. 'Think he can get away from me, does he?' she muttered. 'Well he can't.'

By that time, me and the boys were having hysterics. We crowded onto the verandah and watched as Nani rushed down the beach, yelling her endearments at Koro Apirana. 'You come back here, you old paka.' Well of course he wouldn't, so next thing, the old lady scooted over to *my* dinghy. Before I could protest she gunned the outboard motor and roared off after him. All that afternoon they were yelling at each other. Koro Apirana would row to one location after another in the bay, and Nani Flowers would start the motor and roar after him to growl at him. You have to hand it to the old lady, she had brains all right, picking a rowboat with a motor in it. In the end, old Koro Apirana just gave up. He had no chance, really, because Nani Flowers simply tied his boat to hers and pulled him back to the beach, whether he liked it or not.

That was eight years ago, when Kahu was born, but I remember it as if it was yesterday, especially the wrangling that went on between our Koro and Nani Flowers. The trouble was that Koro Apirana could not reconcile his traditional beliefs about Maori leadership and rights with Kahu's birth. By Maori custom, leadership was hereditary and normally the mantle of prestige fell from the eldest son to the eldest son. Except that in this case, there was an eldest daughter.

'She won't be any good to me,' he would mutter. 'No good. I won't have anything to do with her. That Porourangi better have a son next time.'

In the end, whenever Nani Flowers brought the subject up, Koro Apirana would compress his lips, cross his arms, turn his back on her and look elsewhere and not at her.

I was in the kitchen once when this happened. Nani Flowers was making oven bread on the big table, and Koro Apirana was pretending not to hear her, so she addressed herself to me.

'Thinks he knows everything,' she muttered, tossing her head in Koro Apirana's direction. *Bang*, went her fists into the dough. 'The old paka. Thinks he knows all about being a chief.' *Slap*, went the bread as she threw it on the table. 'He isn't any chief. I'm his chief,' she emphasised to me and, then, over her shoulder to Koro Apirana, 'and don't you forget it either.' *Squelch,* went her fingers as she dug them into the dough.

'Te mea te mea,' Koro Apirana said. 'Yeah, yeah, yeah.'

'Don't you mock *me*,' Nani Flowers responded. *Ouch*, went the bread as she flattened it with her arms. She looked at me grimly and said, 'He *knows* I'm right. He *knows* I'm a descendant of old Muriwai, and *she* was the greatest chief of my tribe. Yeah,' and, *Help*, said the dough as she pummelled it and prodded it and stretched it and strangled it. 'I should have listened to Mum when she told me not to marry him, the old paka,' she said, revving up to her usual climactic pronouncement.

From the corner of my eye I could see Koro Apirana mouthing the words sarcastically to himself.

'But *this* time,' said Nani Flowers, as she throttled the bread with both hands, 'I'm *really* going to divorce him.'

Koro Apirana raised his eyebrows, pretended to be unconcerned.

'Yeah, yeah, yeah,' he said. 'Te mea—'

It was then that Nani Flowers added with a gleam in her eyes, '*And* then I'll go and live with old Waari over the hill.'

I thought to myself, *Uh, oh, I better get out of here*, because Koro Apirana had been jealous of old Waari, who had been Nani Flowers' first boyfriend, for years. No sooner was I out the door when the battle began. *You coward*, said the dough as I ducked.

Four

But that was nothing compared to the fight that they had when Porourangi rang to say he would like to name the baby Kahu.

'What's wrong with Kahu?' Nani Flowers asked.

'I know your tricks,' Koro Apirana said. 'You've been talking to Porourangi behind my back, egging him on.'

This was true, but Nani Flowers said, 'Who, me?' She fluttered her eyelids at the old man.

'You think you're smart,' Koro Apirana said, 'but don't think it'll work.'

This time when he went out to the sea to sulk he took *my* dinghy, the one with the motor in it.

'See if I care,' Nani Flowers said. She had been mean enough, earlier in the day, to siphon out half the petrol so that he couldn't get back. All that afternoon he shouted and waved but she just pretended not to hear. Then Nani Flowers rowed out to him and said that, really, there was nothing he could do. She had telephoned Porourangi and said that the baby could be named Kahu, after Kahutia Te Rangi.

I could understand, however, why the old man was so against the idea. Not only was Kahutia Te Rangi a man's name but it was also the name of the ancestor of our village. Koro Apirana felt that naming a girl-child after the founder of our tribe was belittling Kahutia Te Rangi's prestige. From that time onward, whenever Koro Apirana went past the meeting house, he would look up at the figure of Kahutia Te Rangi on the whale and shake his head sorrowfully. Then he would say to Nani Flowers,

'You stepped out of line, dear, you shouldn't have done it.' To give credit to her, Nani Flowers did appear penitent.

I guess the trouble was that Nani Flowers was always 'stepping out of line'. Even though she had married into our tribe she always made constant reference to her ancestor, Muriwai, who had come to New Zealand on the Maataatua canoe. When the canoe approached Whakatane, which is a long way from our village, Muriwai's chieftainly brothers, lead by Toroa, went to investigate the land. While they were away, however, the sea began to rise and the current carried the canoe so close to the rocks that Muriwai knew all on board would surely perish. So she chanted special prayers, asking the gods to give her the right and open the way for her to take charge. Then she cried, 'E-i! Tena, kia whakatane ake au i ahau!' *Now I shall make myself a man.* She called out to the crew and ordered them to start paddling quickly, and the canoe was saved in the nick of time.

'If Muriwai hadn't done that,' Nani used to say, 'the canoe would have been wrecked.' Then she would hold up her arms and say, 'And I am proud that Muriwai's blood flows in my veins.'

'But that doesn't give you the right,' Koro Apirana said to her one night. He was referring, of course, to her agreeing to the naming of Kahu.

Nani Flowers went up to him and kissed him on the forehead. 'E Koro,' she said softly, 'I have said prayers about it. What's done is done.'

Looking back, I suspect that Nani Flowers' action only helped to harden Koro Apirana's heart against his first-born great-grandchild. But Nani was keeping something back from the old man.

'It's not Porourangi who wants to name the girl Kahu,' she told me. 'It's Rehua.' Then she confided to me that there had been complications in the birth of Kahu and, as a result, the delivery had been by Caesarean section. Rehua, weak and frightened after the birth, had wanted to honour her husband by choosing a name from his people, not hers. That way, should she die, at least her first-born child would be linked to her father's people and land. Rehua was from the same tribe as Nani Flowers and had that same Muriwai blood, so no wonder she got her way with Porourangi.

Then came a third telephone call from Porourangi. Rehua was still in intensive care and Porourangi had to stay with her, but apparently she wanted Kahu's afterbirth, including the birth cord, to be put in the earth on the marae in our village. An auntie of ours would bring the birth cord back to Gisborne on the plane the next day.

Koro Apirana was steadfast in his opposition to Kahu.

'She is of Porourangi's blood and yours,' Nani Flowers said to him. 'It is her right to have her birth cord here on this ground.'

'Then you do it,' Koro Apirana said.

So it was that Nani Flowers sought my help. The next day was Friday, and she got dressed in her formal black clothes and put a scarf over her grey hair. 'Rawiri, I want you to take me to the town,' she said.

I got a bit worried at that because Nani wasn't exactly a featherweight, but she seemed so tense. 'All right,' I said. So I got my motorbike out of the shed, showed her how to sit on the pillion, put my Headhunters jacket on her to keep her warm, and off we roared. As we were going along Wainui Beach some of the other boys joined us. I thought, 'I'll give Nani Flowers a thrill and do a drag down the main street.'

Well, Nani just loved it. There she was, being escorted through the Friday crowd like royalty, waving one hand at everybody and holding on tightly with the other. We had to stop at the lights at Peel Street, and the boys and

I gunned our motors, just for her. Some of Nani's old cronies were crossing; when they saw her through the blue smoke, they almost swallowed their false teeth.

'Oh my goodness,' they said. 'Who is this?'

She smiled supremely. 'I am the Queen of the Headhunters.' At that stage I was getting worried about my shock absorbers, but I couldn't help feeling proud of Nani. Just as we roared off again she poked out her little finger, as if she was having a cup of tea, and said, 'Ta ta.'

But when she met Auntie at the airport, Nani Flowers' mood changed. We were watching from the road when Auntie got off the plane. She started to cry, and then Nani started to cry also. They must have been crying for at least ten minutes before our Auntie passed Kahu's birth cord to Nani. Then Auntie escorted Nani over to us and kissed us all and waved goodbye.

'Take me back to Whangara a quiet way,' Nanni asked. 'I don't want people in the town to see me crying.'

So it was that Nani and I and the boys returned to the village, and Nani was still grieving.

She said to me, 'Rawiri, you and the boys will have to help me. Your grandfather won't come. You're the men who belong to Whangara.'

The night was falling quickly. We followed Nani as she went back and forth across the space in front of the meeting house. She took a quick look around to make sure no one was watching us. The sea hissed and surged through her words.

'This is where the birth cord will be placed,' she said, 'in sight of Kahutia Te Rangi, after whom Kahu has been named. May he, the great ancestor, always watch over her. And may the sea from whence he came always protect her through life.'

Nani Flowers began to scoop a hole in the loose soil. As she placed the birth cord in it, she said a prayer. When she finished, it had grown dark.

She said, 'You boys are the only ones who know where Kahu's birth cord has been placed. It is your secret and mine. You have become her guardians.'

Nani led us to a tap to wash our hands and sprinkle ourselves with water. Just as we were going through the gate we saw the light go on in Koro Apirana's room, far away. I heard Nani whisper in the dark, 'Never mind, Kahu. You'll show him when you grow up. You'll fix the old paka.'

I looked back at the spot where Kahu's birth cord had been placed. At that moment the moon came out and shone full upon the carved figure of Kahutia Te Rangi on his whale.

I saw something flying through the air. It looked like a small spear.

Then, far out to sea, I heard a whale sounding.

Hui e, haumi e, *taiki e*.

Let it be done.

Summer

Halcyon's Flight

Five

Four hundred leagues from Easter Island. Te Pito o te Whenua. Diatoms of light shimmered in the cobalt-blue depths of the Pacific. The herd, sixty strong, led by its ancient leader, was following the course computed by him in the massive banks of his memory. The elderly females assisted the younger mothers, shepherding the newborn in the first journey from the cetacean crib. Way out in front, on point and in the rear, the young males kept guard on the horizon. They watched for danger, not from other creatures of the sea, but from the greatest threat of all – man. At every sighting they would send their ululation back to their leader. They had grown to rely on his memory of the underwater cathedrals where they could take sanctuary, often for days, until man had passed. Such a huge cathedral lay beneath the sea at the place known as the Navel of the Universe.

Yet it had not always been like this, the ancient whale remembered. Once, he had a golden master who had wooed him with flute song. Then his master had used a conch shell to bray his commands to the whale over long distances. As their communication grew so did their understanding and love of each other. Although the young whale had then been almost twelve metres long, his golden master had begun to swim with him in the sea.

Then, one day, his master impetuously mounted him and became the whale rider. In ecstasy the young male had sped out to deep water and, not hearing the cries of fear from his master, had suddenly sounded in a steep accelerated dive, his tail stroking the sky. In that first sounding he had almost killed the one other creature he loved.

Reminiscing like this the ancient bull whale began to cry his grief in sound ribbons of overwhelming sorrow. Nothing that the elderly females could do would stop his sadness. When the younger males reported a man-sighting on the horizon it took all their strength of reasoning to prevent their leader from arrowing out towards the source of danger. Indeed, only after great coaxing were they able to persuade him to lead them to the underwater sanctuary. Even so, they knew with a sense of inevitability that the old one had already begun to sound to the source of his sadness and into the disturbing dreams of his youth.

Six

Three months after Kahu's birth her mother, Rehua, died. Porourangi brought her and Kahu back to our village where the funeral was held. When Rehua's mother asked if she and her people could raise Kahu, Nani Flowers objected strongly. But Porourangi said, 'Let her go,' and Koro Apirana said, 'Yes, let it be as Porourangi wishes,' and thereby overruled her.

A week later, Rehua's mother took Kahu from us. I was there when it happened. Although Porourangi was in tears, Nani was strangely tranquil. She held Kahu close, a small face like a dolphin, held and kissed her.

'Never mind, girl,' she said to baby Kahu. 'Your birth cord is here. No matter where you may go, you will always return. You will never be lost to us.' Then I marvelled at her wisdom and Rehua's in naming the child in our genealogy and the joining of her to our lands.

Our genealogy, of course, is the genealogy of the people of Te Tai Rawhiti, the people of the East Coast; Te Tai Rawhiti actually means 'the place washed by the eastern tide'. Far away beyond the horizon is Hawaiki, our ancestral island homeland, the place of the Ancients and the Gods, and the other side of the world. In between is the huge seamless marine continent which we call Te Moana Nui a Kiwa, the Great Ocean of Kiwa.

The first of the Ancients and ancestors had come from the east, following the pathways in the ocean made by the morning sun. In our case, our ancestor was Kahutia Te Rangi, who was a high chief in Hawaiki. In those days man had power over the creatures of land and sea, and it was Kahutia Te Rangi who travelled here on the back of a whale. This is why our meeting house has a carving of Kahutia Te Rangi on a whale at the apex. It announces our pride in our ancestor and acknowledges his importance to us.

At the time there were already people living in this land, earlier voyagers who had come by canoe. But the land had not been blessed so that it would flower and become fruitful. Other tribes in Aotearoa have their own stories of the high chiefs and priests who then arrived to bless their tribal territories; our blessing was brought by similar chiefs and priests, and Kahutia Te Rangi was one of them. He came riding through the sea astride his whale, and he brought with him the life-giving forces which would enable us to live in close communion with the world. The life-giving forces, in the form of spears, were brought from the Houses of Learning called Te Whakaeroero, Te Rawheoro, Rangitane, and Tapere Nui a Whatonga. They were the gifts of those houses in Hawaiki to the new land. They were very special because, among other things, they gave instructions on how man might talk with the beasts and creatures of the sea so that all could live in helpful partnership. They taught *oneness.*

Kahutia Te Rani landed at Ahuahu, just outside our village, in the early hours of the morning. To commemorate his voyage he was given another name, Paikea. At the time of landfall the star Poututerangi was just rising above our sacred mountain, Hikurangi. The landscape reminded Paikea of his birthplace back in Hawaiki so he named his new home Whangara Mai Tawhiti, which we call Whangara for short. All the other places around here are also named after similar headlands and mountains and rivers in Hawaiki – Tawhiti Point, the Waiapu River, and Tihirau Mai Tawhiti.

It was in this land that Paikea's destiny lay. He married the daughter of Te Whironui, and they were fruitful and

23

had many sons and grandsons. And the people lived on the lands around his home at Ranginui, cultivating their sweet potato and vegetable gardens in peace and holding fast to the heritage of their ancestors.

Four generations later came the great ancestor Porourangi, after whom my eldest brother is named. Under his leadership the descent lines of all the people of Te Tai Rawhiti were united in what is now known as the Ngati Porou confederation. His younger brother, Tahu Potiki, founded the South Island's Kai Tahu confederation.

Many centuries later, the chieftainship was passed to Koro Apirana and, from him, to my brother Porourangi. Then Porourangi had a daughter whom he named Kahu.

That was eight years ago, when Kahu was born and then taken to live with her mother's people. I doubt if any of us realised how significant she would become in our lives. When a child is growing up somewhere else you can't see the small signs which mark her out as different, someone with a destiny. As I have said before, we were all looking somewhere else.

Eight years ago I was sixteen. I'm twenty-four now. The boys and I still kick around and, although some of my girlfriends have tried hard to tempt me away from it, my first love is still my BSA. Once a bikie always a bikie. Looking back, I can truthfully say that Kahu was never forgotten by me and the boys. After all, we were the ones who brought her birth cord back to Whangara, and only we and Nani Flowers knew where it was buried. We were Kahu's guardians; whenever I was near the place of her birth cord, I would feel a little tug at my motorbike jacket and a voice saying, 'Hey Uncle Rawiri, don't forget me.' I told Nani Flowers about it once and her eyes glistened. 'Even though Kahu is a long way from us she's letting us know she's thinking of us. One of these days she'll come back.'

24

As it happened, Pourourangi went up to get her and bring her back for a holiday the following summer. At that time he had returned from the South Island to live in Whangara but to work in the city. Koro Apirana was secretly pleased with this arrangement because he had been wanting to pass on his knowledge to Pourourangi. One of these days my eldest brother will be the big chief. All of a sudden, during a cultural practice in the meeting house, Pourourangi looked up at our ancestor Paikea and said to Koro Apirana, 'I am feeling very lonely for my daughter.' Koro Apirana didn't say a word, probably hoping that Pourourangi would forget his loneliness. Nani Flowers, however, as quick as a flash, said, 'Oh, you poor thing. You better go up and bring her back for a nice holiday with her grandfather.' We knew she was having a sly dig at Koro Apirana. We could also tell that *she* was lonely, too, for the grandchild who was so far away from her.

On Kahu's part, when she first met Koro Apirana, it must have been love at first sight because she dribbled all over him. Pourourangi had walked through the door with his daughter and Nani Flowers, cross-eyed with joy, had grabbed Kahu for a great big hug. Then she put Kahu in Koro Apirana's arms before he could say 'No'.

'Oh, no,' Koro Apirana said.

'A little dribbling never hurt anybody,' Nani Flowers scoffed.

'That's not the end I'm worried about,' he grumbled, lifting up Kahu's blankets. We had to laugh, because Kahu had dribbled at that end, too.

Looking back, I have to say that that first family reunion with Kahu was filled with warmth and love. It was surprising how closely Kahu and Koro Apirana resembled each other. The only difference was that she loved him but he didn't love her. He gave her back to Nani Flowers and she started to cry, reaching for him. But he turned away and walked out of the house.

'Never mind, Kahu,' Nani Flowers crooned. 'He'll come around.' The trouble was, though, that he never did.

I suppose there were many reasons for Koro Apirana's attitude. For one thing, both he and Nani Flowers were in their seventies and, although Nani Flowers still loved grandchildren, Koro Apirana was probably tired of them. For another, he was the big chief of the tribe and was perhaps more preoccupied with the many serious issues facing the survival of the Maori people and our land. But most of all, he had not wanted an eldest girl-child in Kahu's generation; he had wanted an eldest boy-child, somebody more appropriate to teach the traditions of the village to. We didn't know it at the time, but he had already begun to look in other families for such a boy-child.

Kahu didn't know this either so, of course, her love for him remained steadfast. Whenever she saw him she would try to sit up and to dribble some more to attract his attention.

'That kid's hungry,' Koro Apirana would say.

'Yeah,' Nani Flowers would turn to us, 'she's hungry for *him*, the old paka. Hungry for his love. Come to think of it, I must get a divorce and find a young husband.' She and all of us would try to win Kahu over to us but, no, the object of her affection remained a bald man with no teeth.

At that time there was still nothing about Kahu which struck us as out of place. But then two small events occurred. The first was when we discovered that Kahu adored the Maori food. Nani had given her a spoonful of fermented corn, and next minute Kahu had eaten the lot. 'This kid's a throwback,' Nani Flowers said. 'She doesn't like milk or hot drinks, only cold water. She doesn't like sugar, only Maori food.'

The second event happened one night when Koro Apirana was having a tribal meeting at the house. He had asked all the men to be there, including me and the boys.

26

We crowded into the sitting room and after prayer and a welcome speech, he got down to business. He said he wanted to begin a regular instruction period for the men so that we would be able to learn our history and our customs. Just the men, he added, because men were sacred. Of course the instruction wouldn't be like in the old days, not as strict, but the purpose would be the same: to keep the Maori language going, and to increase the strength of the tribe. It was important, he said, for us to be so taught. The lessons would be held in the meeting house and would begin the following week.

Naturally we all agreed. Then, in the relaxed atmosphere that always occurs after a serious discussion, Koro Apirana told us of his own instruction years ago under the guidance of a priest. One story followed another, and we were all enthralled because the instruction had mainly taken the form of tests or challenges which he had to pass: tests of memory, as in remembering long lines of genealogy; tests of dexterity, wisdom, physical and psychological strength. Among them had been a dive into deep water to retrieve a carved stone dropped there by the priest.

'There were so many tests,' said Koro Apirana, 'and some of them I did not understand. But I do know the old man had the power to talk to the beasts and creatures of the sea. Alas, we have lost that power now. Finally, near the end of my training, he took me into his hut. He put out his foot and pointing to the big toe, said "Bite." So I did, and—'

Suddenly, Koro Apirana broke off. A look of disbelief spread over his face. Trembling, he peered under the table, and so did we. Kahu was there. Somehow she had managed to crawl unobserved into the room. Koro Apirana's toes must have looked juicy to her because there she was, biting on his big toe and making small snarling sounds as she played with it, like a puppy with

27

a bone. Then she looked up at him, and her eyes seemed to say, 'Don't think you've leaving *me* out of this.'

We were laughing when we told Nani Flowers.

'I don't know what's so funny,' she said sarcastically, 'Kahu could have gotten poisoned. But good on her to take a bite at the old man.'

Koro Apirana, however, was not so amused and now I understand why.

Seven

The next time Kahu came to us she was two years old. She came with Porourangi, who had a lovely woman called Ana with him. It looked like they were in love. But Nani Flowers had eyes only for Kahu.

'Thank goodness,' Nani Flowers said after she had embraced Kahu, 'you've grown some hair.'

Kahu giggled. She had turned into a bright button-eyed little girl with shining skin. She wanted to know where her great-grandfather was.

'The old paka,' said Nani Flowers. 'He's been in Wellington on Maori Council business. But he comes back on the bus tonight. We'll go and pick him up.'

We had to smile, really, because Kahu was so eager to see Koro Apirana. She wriggled and squirmed all the way into town. We bought her a soft drink but she didn't want it, preferring water instead. Then, when the bus arrived and Koro Apirana stepped off with other Council officials, she ran at him with a loud, infectious joy in her voice. I guess we should have expected it, but it was still a surprise to hear her greeting to him. For his part, he stood there thunderstruck, looking for somewhere to hide.

Oh, the shame, the embarrassment, as she flung herself into his arms, crying, 'Oh *Paka*. You home now, you *Paka*. Oh, *Paka*.'

He blamed us all for that, and he tried to persuade Kahu to call him 'Koro', but *Paka* he was, and *Paka* he became forever after.

* * *

Being a big chief, Koro Apirana was often called to meetings all over the country to represent us. He had the reputation of being stern and tyrannical and because of this many people were afraid of him. 'Huh,' Nani Flowers used to say, 'they should face *me* and then they'll know all about it.' But me and the boys had a grudging admiration for the old fella. He might not always be fair but he was a good fighter for the Maori people. Our pet name for our Koro was 'Super Maori' and, even now, telephone boxes still remind me of him. We used to joke: 'If you want help at Bastion Point, call Super Maori. If you want a leader for your Land March, just dial Whangara 214K. If you want a man of strength at a Waitangi protest, phone the Maori Man of Steel.' Mind you, he wasn't on our side when we protested against the Springbok Tour but then that just shows you the kind of man he was: his own boss. 'Right or wrong,' Nani Flowers would add.

The meeting that Koro Apirana had attended was about the establishment of Kohanga Reo, or language nests, where young children could learn the Maori language. The adult version was the language school, the regular instruction of the kind which Koro Apirana had established a year before in Whangara. Although we weren't that well educated, the boys and I enjoyed the lessons every weekend. It soon became obvious that Kahu did, also. She would sneak up to the door of the meeting house and stare in at us.

'Go away,' Koro Apirana would thunder. Quick as a flash Kahu's head would bob away. But slowly we would see it again, like a spiny sea urchin. I suspect that Kahu overheard more than we thought. I am certain she must have been there when we learnt that man was once able to talk, to communicate, with whales. After all, Paikea must have had to tell his whale where to come.

* * *

The whale has always held a special place in the order of things, even before those times of Paikea. That was way back, after the Sky Father and Earth Mother had been separated, when the God children of both parents divided up between themselves the various Kingdoms of the Earth. It was the Lord Tangaroa who took the Kingdom of the Ocean; he was second in rank only to the Lord Tane, the Father of Man and the Forests, and so was established by them the close kinship of man with the inhabitants of the ocean, and of land with sea. This was the first communion.

Then the Lord Tangaroa appointed the triad of Kiwa, Rona and Kaukau to assist his sovereign rule: Kiwa to be guardian of the southern ocean, Rona to help control the tides, and Kaukau to aid the welfare of the sea's denizens. To the triad, two other guardians from the Kingdom of the Land, Takaaho and Te Pu-whakahara, brought a special suit: their offspring had been given lakes to live in, but they preferred to roam the freedom of the sea. The suit was accepted, and this was how sharks and whales were granted habitation of the ocean.

From the very beginning the whale was grateful for this release and this was why the whale family, the Wehenga-kauiki, became known as the helpers of men lost at sea. Whenever asked, the whale would attend the call, as long as the mariner possessed the necessary authority and knew the way of talking to whales.

But as the world aged and man grew away from his godliness, he began to lose the power of speech with whales, the power of *interlock*. So it was that the knowledge of whalespeaking was given only to a few. One of these was our ancestor, Paikea.

Then came the time when Paikea asked his whale to bring him to our land, far to the south, and it was done.

As for the whale itself, some people say the whale was transformed into an island; viewed from the highway to

31

Tolaga Bay, the island certainly *does* look like a whale breaking through the water.

The years went by, and the descendants of Paikea increased on the land and always paid homage to their ancestor and the whale island. In those days there was still communion with the Gods and a close relationship between land inhabitants and ocean inhabitants. Whenever man wished to cross the border between his kingdom and that of the ocean he would honour Tangaroa by making offerings of seaweed, fish or birds. And when Tangaroa granted man good fishing, man would return the first fish of the catch to the sea god as acknowledgement that his welfare was only by leave of Tangaroa. So it was that ceremonials of respect were employed between man and sea. For instance, fishing was sacred and women therefore did not go out with the men, and fishing grounds became steeped in special rituals to ensure their bounty. And even the shark, in those days, was a helper to man unless man had transgressed a sacred law.

Until the time came when man turned on the beast which had been companion to him and the whalekilling began.

That night, after the school on the whales, I arrived home to find Nani Flowers out on the verandah with Kahu in her arms, rocking back and forth, back and forth.

'Rawiri, what happened down there?' she asked, jerking her head at the meeting house. I saw Kahu rubbing small fists against her eyes.

'Nothing,' I answered. 'Why?'

'This kid has been sobbing her heart out,' Nani Flowers said. She paused. 'Did the old paka growl at her?'

Ever since the school had started, Nani Flowers had been hassling Koro Apirana. While she agreed that the instruction should take place, she couldn't help feeling

32

affronted about the exclusion of women. 'Them's the rules,' Koro Apirana had told her. 'I know, but rules are made to be broken,' she had replied in a huff. So, every first Saturday of the month, she would start to play up and pick on Koro Apirana. 'Yeah, yeah, yeah,' he would say. 'Te mea te mea.'

'He didn't growl at Kahu any more than usual,' I answered. 'He just doesn't like her hanging around when we have the school, that's all.'

Nani Flowers compressed her lips. I could tell that rebellion was ready to boil over inside her. Then she said to me, 'Well you take this kid with you somewhere because I'm going to have a word with Koro Api when he gets back, the old paka.'

I must admit that I was brassed off, having Kahu shoved at me like that. I was planning on taking my darling Cheryl Marie to the movies. So I phoned her up to explain that I had to look after a baby.

'Oh yeah,' Cheryl said sarcastically. 'And I suppose she's not five foot two with eyes of blue.' Cheryl was jealous of my other friend, Rhonda Anne.

'No,' I said. 'My baby is *you*. Eyes of brown and lives in town.'

Would you believe it, Cheryl hung up on me? So what else could I do except take Kahu to the movies instead. The boys laughed when I zoomed up to the Majestic with my substitute 'date' under my leather jacket, but the girls loved her. 'Oh, isn't she gorgeous? Isn't she sweet?' Yuck. I could see a mile off that the girls were also assessing whether I had now become marrying material. No *way*.

The movie had already started. Children weren't supposed to see it, but the darkness made it easier to sneak Kahu in. What I hadn't realised, however, was that the main feature was about a whale being hunted through Antarctic waters. Everything was fine, really, for most of the film, because Kahu soon fell asleep. Having her curled up so close to me made me feel protective, like a father, I guess, and I think my bonding to her was confirmed that night.

I felt I should look after her till the world ended; every now and then, I would open my jacket and sneak a look at her tiny face, so wan in the light of the flickering film. And a lump would come to my throat and I would think to myself, 'No, Kahu, I won't forget you, ever.'

Then the final tragedy of the movie began. The whale, wounded, was dying in its own blood. The soundtrack was suddenly filled with the sound of the whale in its death throes: long, echoing, sighing phrases which must have been recorded from real whales. The sound was strange and utterly sad. No wonder when I looked at Kahu she had woken from sleep, and tears were again tracking down her face. Not even a lolly would help to pacify her.

Nani Flowers and Koro Apirana had finished their argument by the time I returned home, but the atmosphere was as frozen as the Antarctic wasteland in the film.

'He's sleeping in the bunkhouse with you tonight,' Nani Flowers told me, jerking her head at Koro Apirana. 'I've had enough of him. Divorce tomorrow, I mean it this time.' Then she remembered something and after taking Kahu from me, twisted my ear. *Ouch*. 'And that'll teach you to take my great-grandchild out all night and all over the place. I've been scared to death. Where'd you go?'

'To the movies.'

'To a *picture*?' *Bang* came her open hand over my head. 'And *then* where!'

'Down to the beach.'

'The *beach*?' I ducked her hand, but *kick* came her foot to my behind. 'Don't you do that again!' She hugged Kahu tightly and took her into hers and Koro Apirana's bedroom and *slam* went the door.

I thought of Cheryl Marie. 'Looks like both of us lucked out tonight,' I said to Koro Apirana.

Half way through the night I suddenly remembered something. I tried to wake Koro Apirana, snoring beside me, but he only tried to snuggle up to me, saying, 'Flowers, darling wife . . .' So I edged away from him quickly and sat there, staring through the window at the glowing moon.

I had wanted to tell Koro Apirana that on our way back from the movie, the boys and I had gone up to the Point at Sponge Bay. The sea had looked like crinkled silver foil smoothed right out to the edge of the sky.

'Hey!' one of the boys had said, pointing. 'Over there. Orca!'

It had been uncanny, really, seeing those killer whales slicing stealthily through the sea, uncanny and disturbing as a dream.

Even more strange, though, was that Kahu had begun to make eerie sounds in her throat. I swear that those long lamenting sighs of hers were exactly the same as I had heard in the movie theatre. It sounded as if she was warning them.

The orca suddenly dived.

Hui e, haumi e, *taiki e*.

Let it be done.

Eight

The following summer, when Kahu was three, was dry and dusty on the Coast. Koro Apirana was concerned about our drinking water and was considering at one point bringing it in by road tanker. One of the boys suggested that the sweetest water was DB light brown and that the hotel up at Tatapouri would be happy to deliver it free. Another of the boys added that we'd have to escort it to Whangara because, for sure, someone would want to hijack it.

Into all this rough and tumble of our lives, Kahu brought a special radiance. Koro Apirana was as grumpy with her as ever but, now that Porourangi was home and the school sessions were attracting young boys for him to teach, he seemed to bear less of a grudge against her for being a girl and the eldest grandchild.

'Don't blame Kahu,' Nani Flowers used to growl. 'If your blood can't beat my Muriwai blood that's your tough luck.'

'Te mea te mea,' Koro Apirana would reply. 'Yeah, yeah, yeah.'

In particular, Koro Apirana had discovered three sons from royal bloodlines to whom he hoped to pass the mantle of knowledge. And from the corner of his eye, he could see that Porourangi and his new girlfriend, Ana, were growing very fond of each other. Now *she* didn't have any Muriwai blood so, you never knew, Porourangi might come up with a son yet.

Under these conditions, the love which Kahu received from Koro Apirana was the sort that dropped off the edge of the table, like breadcrumbs after everybody else has had a big meal. But Kahu didn't seem to mind. She ran into Koro Apirana's arms whenever he had time for her and took whatever he was able to give. If he had told her he loved dogs I'm sure she would have barked, 'Woof woof.' That's how much she loved him.

Summer is always shearing season for us and that summer the boys and I got a contract to shear sheep for the local farmers around the Coast. On the first few mornings when Kahu was at home I would see her staring at us over the window sill as we left. Her eyes seemed to say, 'Hey, don't forget about me, Uncle Rawiri.' So one morning I made her life happy.

'I think I'll take Kahu to work with me,' I said to Nani Flowers.

'Oh, no you don't,' Nani Flowers said. 'She'll get hurt.'

'No. No. She'll be all right. Eh, Kahu?'

Kahu's eyes were shining. 'Oh, *yes*. Can I go, Nani?'

'All right then,' Nani Flowers grumbled. 'But tomorrow you have to be my helper in the vegetable garden. Okay?'

So it was that Kahu became the mascot for me and the boys and it only seemed natural, after a while, for us to take her with us wherever we went – well, most places anyway, and only when Nani Flowers didn't want her to help in the garden.

But that first night I was in big trouble with the old lady.

'*Hoi*,' she said, and *bang* came her hand. 'What did you do with Kahu at work? She's tuckered out.'

'Nothing,' I squealed. *Biff* came her fist at my stomach. 'She just helped us shear the sheep and sweep the floors and press the wool and—'

Swish came the broom. 'Yeah,' Nani Flowers said. 'And I'll bet all you bums were just lying back and having a good *smoke*.'

You could never win with Nani Flowers.

* * *

37

At that time the school sessions were proving to be very popular. All of us felt the need to understand more about our roots. But Nani Flowers still grumbled whenever we had our gathering. She would sit with Kahu in her arms, rocking in the chair on the verandah, watching the men walk past.

'There go the Ku Klux Klan,' she would say loudly so that we could all hear.

Poor Kahu, she could never keep away from our school. She would always try to listen in at the doorway to the meeting house.

'Go away,' Koro Apirana would thunder. But there was one school that Kahu could not eavesdrop on, and that was the one which Koro Apirana led when he took us out in a small flotilla of fishing boats to have a lesson on the sea.

'In our village,' Koro Apirana told us, 'we have always endeavoured to live in harmony with Tangaroa's kingdom and the guardians therein. We have made offerings to the sea god to thank him and when we need his favour, and we have called upon our guardians whenever we are in need of help. We have blessed every new net and new line to Tangaroa. We have tried not to take food with us in our boats when we fish because of the sacred nature of our task.'

The flotilla was heading out to sea.

'Our fishing areas have always been placed under the protective custody of the guardians,' Koro Apirana said. 'In their honour we have often placed talismanic shrines. In this way the fish have been protected and attracted to the fishing grounds, and thus a plentiful supply has been assured. We try never to overfish for to do so would be to take greedy advantage of Tangaroa and would bring retribution.'

Then we reached the open sea and Koro Apirana motioned that we should stay close to him.

'All of our fishing grounds, banks and rocks have had names assigned to them and the legends surrounding them have been commemorated in story, song, or proverb. Where our fishing grounds have no local identification, like a reef or upjutting rock, we have taken the *fix* from prominent cliffs or mountains on the shore. Like *there* and *mark*. And *there* and *mark*. In this way the fishing places of all our fish species have always been known. And we have tried never to trespass on the fishing grounds of others because *their* guardians would recognise us as interlopers. In this respect, should we ever be in unfamiliar sea, we have surrounded ourselves with our own water for protection.'

Then Koro Apirana's voice dropped and, when he resumed his lesson, his words were stepped with sadness and regret. 'But we have not always kept our pact with Tangaroa, and in these days of commercialism it is not always easy to resist temptation. So it was when I was your age. So it is now. There are too many people with snorkelling gear, and too many commercial fishermen with licences. We have to place prohibitions on our fishing beds, boys, otherwise it will be just like the whales—'

For a moment Koro Apirana hesitated. Far out to sea there was a dull booming sound like a great door opening, a reminder, a memory of something downward plunging. Koro Apirana shaded his eyes from the sun.

'Listen, boys,' he said, and his voice was haunted. 'Listen. Once there were many of our protectors. Now there are few. *Listen how empty our sea has become.*'

In the evening after our lesson on the sea we assembled in the meeting house. The booming on the open waters had heralded the coming of a rainstorm. As I went into the meeting house I glanced up at our ancestor, Paikea. He looked like he was lifting his whale through the spearing rain.

Koro Apirana led us in a prayer to bless the school. Then, after the introductions, he told us of the times which had brought the silence to the sea.

'I was a boy of seven years' age,' he began, 'when I went to stay with my uncle who was a whaler. I was too young to know any better, and I didn't understand then, as I do now, about our ancestor, the whale. At that time whaling was one of the great pastimes and once the bell on the lookout had been sounded you'd see all the whaling boats tearing out to sea, chasing after a whale. Doesn't matter what you were doing, you'd drop everything, your plough, your sheep clippers, your schoolbooks, *everything*. I can still remember seeing everyone climbing the lookout, like white balloons. I followed them and far out to sea I saw a herd of whales.'

The rain fell through his words. 'They were the most beautiful sight I had ever seen.' He made a sweeping gesture. 'Then, down by the slipway, I could see the longboats being launched into the sea. I ran down past the sheds, and the pots on the fires were already being stoked to boil down the blubber. All of a sudden my uncle yelled out to me to get on his boat with him. So there I was, heading out to sea.'

I saw a spiky head sneaking a look through the door. 'That's when I saw the whales really close,' Koro Apirana said. 'There must have been sixty of them at least. I have never forgotten, never. They had prestige. They were so powerful. Our longboat got so close to one that I was able to reach out and touch the skin.' His voice was hushed with awe. 'I felt the ripple of power beneath the skin. It felt like silk. Like a god. Then the harpoons began to sing through the air. But I was young, you see, and all I could feel was the thrill, like when you do a haka.'

He paused, mesmerised. 'I can remember that when a whale was harpooned it would fight with all its strength. Eventually it would spout blood like a fountain, and the sea would be red. Three or four other boats would tow it ashore to the nearest place and cut it up and share out the meat and the oil and everything. When we started to strip the blubber off the whale in the whaling station, all the blood flowed into the channel. Blind eels would come up with the tide to drink the blood.'

I heard Kahu weeping at the doorway. I edged over to her and when she saw me she put her arms around my neck.

'You better go home,' I whispered, 'before Koro Apirana finds out you're here.'

But she was so frightened. She was making a mewling sound in her throat. She seemed paralysed with terror.

Inside, Koro Apirana was saying, 'When it was all finished we would cut huge slabs of whale meat and sling them across our horses and take them to our homes—'

Suddenly, before I could stop her, Kahu wrenched away from me and ran into the meeting house.

'No, Paka, *no!*' she screamed.

His mouth dropped open. 'Haere atu koe! Get away from here,' he shouted.

'Paka. Paka, no!'

Grimly, Koro Apirana walked up to her, took her by the arms and virtually hurled her out. 'Go. Get away from here,' he repeated. The sea thundered ominously. The rain fell like spears.

Kahu was still crying three hours later. Nani Flowers was livid when she heard about what happened.

'You just keep her away from the meeting house,' Koro Apirana said. 'That's all I say. I've told you before. *And* her.'

'My blame,' Kahu wept. 'Love Paka.'

'You *men*,' Nani Flowers said. 'I can show *you* where you come from.'

'Enough,' Koro Apirana said. He stormed out and that ended the argument.

Later that night Kahu kept sobbing and sobbing. I guess we thought she was still grieving about being yelled at, but we know better now. I heard Nani Flowers going into Kahu's bedroom and comforting her.

'Slide over, Kahu,' Nani Flowers soothed. 'Make a little space for your skinny Nani. There, there.'

'Love Paka.'

'You can *have* him, Kahu, as soon as I get my divorce tomorrow. There, there.' Nani was really hurting with love for Kahu. 'Don't you worry, don't you worry. You'll fix him up, the old paka, when you get older.'

Over the hiss and roar of the surf I listened to Nani Flowers. After a short while Kahu drifted off to sleep.

'Yes,' Nani Flowers crooned, 'go to sleep now. And if you don't fix him,' she whispered, 'then I swear I will.'

Hiss and roar. Ebb and flow.

The next morning I sneaked in to give Kahu a special cuddle, just from me. When I opened the door she was gone. I looked in Koro Apirana and Nani Flowers' bedroom, but she wasn't there either. Nani Flowers had pushed Koro onto the floor and had spread herself over the whole bed to make sure he couldn't get back in.

Outside the sea was gentle and serene, as if the storm had never happened. In the clear air I heard a chittering, chatter sound from the beach. I saw Kahu far away, silhouetted on the sand. She was standing facing the sea, listening to voices in the surf. *There, there, Kahu. There, there*.

Suddenly Kahu turned and saw me. She ran toward me like a seagull. 'Uncle Rawiri!'

I saw three silver shapes leaping into the dawn.

Autumn

Season of the Sounding Whale

Nine

If you ask me the name of this house, I shall tell you. It is Te Kani. And the carved figure at the apex? It is Paikea, it is Paikea. Paikea swam. The sea god swam. The sea monster swam. And Paikea, you landed at Ahuahu. You changed into Kahutia Te Rangi. You gave your embrace to the daughter of Te Whironui, who sat in the stern of the canoe. And now you are a carved figurehead, old man.

The sea trench, Hawaiki. The Place of the Gods. The Home of the Ancients. The whale herd hovered in the goldened sea like regal airships. Far above, the surface of the sea was afire with the sun's plunge from day into night. Below lay the sea trench. The herd was waiting for the sign from their ancient leader that it should descend between the protective walls of the trench and flow with the thermal stream away from the island known as the Place of the Gods.

But their leader was still mourning. Two weeks earlier the herd had been feeding in the Tuamotu Archipelago when suddenly a flash of bright light had scaled the sea and giant tidal soundwaves had exerted so much pressure that internal ear canals had bled. Seven young calves had died. The ancient whale remembered this occurrence happening before; screaming a lament of condemnation, he had led them away in front of the lethal tide that he knew would come. On that pellmell, headlong, and mindless escape, he had noticed more cracks in the ocean floor, hairline fractures indicating serious damage below the crust of the earth. Now, some weeks later, the leader was still unsure about the radiation level in the sea trench. He was fearful of the contamination seeping from Moruroa. He was afraid of the genetic effects of the undersea radiation on the remaining herd and calves in this place which had once, ironically, been the womb of the world.

The elderly females tried to nurse his nostalgia, but the ancient whale could not stop the rush of memories. Once this place had been crystal clear. It had been the place of his childhood and that of his golden master, too. Following that first disastrous sounding, they had ridden many times above the trench. His golden master had taught the whale to flex his muscles and sinews so that handholds in the skin would appear, enabling the rider to ascend to the whale's head. There, further muscle contractions would provide saddle and stirrups. And when the whale sounded, he would lock his master's ankles with strong muscles and open a small breathing chamber, just behind his spout. In the space of time, his master needed only to caress his left fin, and the whale would respond.

Suddenly, the sea trench seemed to pulsate and crackle with a lightswarm of luminescence. Sparkling like a galaxy was a net of radioactive death. For the first time in all the years of his leadership, the ancient whale deviated from his usual primeval route. The herd ascended to the surface. The decision was made to seek the silent waters of the Antarctic. But the elderly females pealed their anxieties to one another because the dangerous islands were also in that vicinity. Nevertheless they quickly followed their leader away from the poisoned water. They were right to worry because the ancient whale could only despair that the place of life, and the Gods, had now become a place of death. The herd thundered through the sea.

Haumi e, hui e, taiki e.

Let it be done.

Ten

The next year Kahu turned four and I decided it was about time I went out to see the world. Koro Apirana thought it was a good idea but Nani Flowers didn't like it at all.

'What's wrong with Whangara?' she said. 'You got the whole world right here. Nothing you can get anywhere else that you can't get here. You must be in *trouble*.'

I shook my head. 'No, I'm clean,' I answered.

'Then there must be a girl you're running away from.' She looked at me suspiciously, and poked me between the ribs. 'You been up to mischief, eh?'

I denied that too. Laughing, I eased myself up from the chair and assumed a cowboy stance. 'Let's just say, Ma'am,' I drawled, then went for my six-gun, 'that there's not enough room in this here town for the two of us.'

Over the following four months I put in double time at work and saved up for a plane ticket. The boys took up a collection and gave me a fantastic party. My girlfriend Joyleen Carol cried buckets over me. At the airport I said to Nani Flowers, 'Don't forget to look after my bike.'

'Don't worry,' she said sarcastically, 'I'll feed it some hay and give it water every day.'

'Give Kahu a kiss from me.'

'Ae,' Nani Flowers quivered. 'God be with you. And don't forget to come back, Rawiri, or else—'

She pulled a toy water-pistol from her basket.

'*Bang*,' she said.

I flew to Australia.

* * *

Unlike Kahu, my birth cord couldn't have been put in the ground at Whangara because I didn't return there until four years later. I discovered that everything I'd been told about Australia was true: it was big, bold, brassy, bawdy and beautiful. When I first arrived I stayed in Sydney with my cousin, Kingi, who had an apartment in Bondi. I hadn't realised that there were so many other Maoris over there (I thought I'd be the first) and after a while I realised why it was nicknamed 'Kiwi Valley'. Wherever you went – the pubs, the shows, the clubs, the restaurants, the movies, the theatres – you could always count on bumping into a Maori cousin. In some hotels, above the noise and buzz of the patrons, you were bound to hear somebody shouting to somebody else, 'Gidday, cous!'

I was like a kid in a great big toyshop, wanting to touch everything. Whangara wasn't as big as *this*, with its teeming city streets, glass skyscrapers, glitter and glitz. Nor could Friday night in the town ever compare with the action in the Cross, that part of Sydney to which people thronged, either to look or be looked at. People were selling anything and everything up the Cross, and if you wanted to buy you just 'paid the man'.

It was there I came upon my cous Henare, who was now wearing a dress, and another cous, Reremoana, who had changed her name to Lola L'Amour and had red hair and fishnet stockings. I couldn't understand Kingi's attitude at all; he was always trying to cross the street whenever he saw a cous he didn't want to be seen with. But I would just bowl along regardless and yell, 'Gidday cous!'

As far as I could see, they were living the way they wanted to and no matter what changes they had made to themselves or their lives, a cous was a cous. I guess also that I didn't feel that much different: I looked much the same as they did, with my leather jacket and pants matching their own gear with its buckles and scarves and whips. 'What game are you into?' they would tease. 'What game?' They would joke around and sometimes we would meet up later at some party or other. But always, in the early morning, when the sunlight was beginning to crack the midnight glamour, the memories would come seeping through. 'How's our Nani? How's our Koro? If you write to them, don't tell them that you saw us like *this*.'

In the search for fame, fortune, power and success, some of my cousins had opted for the base metal and not the gold. They may have turned their lives upside down in the process, like Sydney Bridge's reflection in the harbour, but they always craved the respect of our tribe. They weren't embarrassed, but hiding the way they lived was one way of maintaining the respect. There was no better cloak than those starry nights under the turning Southern Cross.

Kingi and I got along fine, but when I made a friend of my own, I moved in with him. I had gotten a job working as a bricklayer and had also started playing Rugby League. It was through League that I met my buddy, Jeff, who told me he was looking for someone to share his flat. Jeff was a friendly guy, quick to laugh, quick to believe, and quick to trust. He told me of his family in Mount Hagen, Papua New Guinea, and I told him about mine in Whangara. I also told him about Kahu.

'You'd love her,' I said. 'She's a fantastic looker. Big brown eyes, wonderful figure and lips just waiting to be kissed.'

'Yeah? Yeah?' he asked eagerly.

'And I can tell she'd go for *you*,' I said. 'She's warm and cuddly, great to be with, and she just loves snuggling up close. And—'

Poor Jeff, he didn't realise I was pulling his leg. And as the weeks went by I embellished the story even more.

I just couldn't help it. But that's how our friendship was; we were always kidding around or kidding each other.

I must have been in Sydney over a year when the phone call came from my brother Porourangi. Sometimes life has a habit of flooding over you and rushing you along in its overwhelming tide. Living in Australia was like that: there was always something going on, day and night. If Jeff and I weren't playing League we'd be out surfing (the beach at Whangara was better) or partying with buddies, or hiking out to the Blue Mountains. You could say I had begun drowning in it all, giving myself up to what Kingi would have called 'the hedonistic life of the lotus eater'. Kingi was always one for the big words. He used to tell me that his favourite image of Australia was of Joan Sutherland singing 'Advance Australia Fair', a can of Fosters in one hand, and surfing supremely into Sydney Harbour like an antipodean Statue of Liberty. See what I mean? All those big words? That's Kingi, for sure.

I was still in bed when the telephone rang, so Jeff answered. Next minute, a pillow came flying at me and Jeff yanked me out of bed saying, 'Phone, Rawiri. And I'll talk to *you* later.'

Well, the *good* news was that Porourangi was getting married to Ana. Nani Flowers had been pestering both of them about it. 'And you know what she's like,' Porourangi laughed. 'Don't bother to come home though,' he said, 'because the wedding is just going to be very small.' Kahu would be the flower girl.

'How is she?' I asked.

'She's five and started school now,' Porourangi said. 'She's still living with Rehua's folks. She missed you very much last summer.'

'Give her a kiss from me,' I said. 'And also kiss our Nani. Tell everybody I love them. How's Koro?'

'In Nani's bad books as usual,' Porourangi laughed. 'The sooner they get a divorce the better.'

I wished Porourangi and Ana the very best with their life together. The season of bereavement had been long over for Porourangi and it was time for renewal. Then just before he hung up, he said, 'Oh, by the way, your flatmate was very interested in Kahu, so I told him she was doing well with her spelling.'

Uh, oh. That was the *bad* news. No sooner had I put the phone down than Jeff laid into me.

'Warm and cuddly, huh?'

'No, wait Jeff, I can explain—'

'Big brown eyes and fantastic figure, huh?'

'Jeff, no—' In his hands he had a soggy apple pie.

'Lips just waiting to be kissed?' He eyes gleamed with vengeance.

I should count myself lucky that I had cooked dinner the night before. Had it been Jeff, that apple pie wouldn't have been so scrumptious.

Not long after that Jeff also got a phone call, but the news wasn't so good. His mother called from Papua New Guinea to ask him to come home.

'Your father's too proud to call himself,' she said, 'but he's getting on, Jeff, and he needs you to help him run the coffee plantation. He's had a run of rotten luck with the workers this year and you know what the natives are like, always drinking.'

'I'll have to go,' said Jeff. I knew he was reluctant to do so. Indeed, one of the reasons why he had come to Sydney was that it was as far from his family as he could get. He loved them deeply, but sometimes love becomes a power game between the ambitions that parents have for their children and the ambitions that children have for themselves. 'But it looks like all my chickens are coming home to roost,' Jeff said ruefully.

'Family is family,' I said.

'Say,' he interrupted. 'You wouldn't like to come with me?'

I hesitated. Ever since speaking to Porourangi I had actually been thinking of going back to New Zealand. Instead, I said, 'Sure, I've been a cowboy all my life. Let's saddle up, partner.' So we started to pack up and get ready to move on out. I called Whangara to tell Nani Flowers.

'You're going *where*?' she yelled. As usual she was holding the phone at arm's length.

'To Papua New Guinea.'

'What!' she said. 'You'll get eaten up by all them cannibals. What's at Papua New Guinea' – I mouthed the words along with her – 'that you can't get in Whangara? You should come home instead of roaming all over the world.'

'I'll be home next summer. I promise.' There was silence at the other end. 'Hullo?'

Koro Apirana came to the phone. 'Rawiri?' he said loudly. 'What did you say? Your Nani is crying.' There was a tussle at the other end and Nani Flowers returned.

'I can speak for myself,' she said in a huff. Then, in a soft voice, full of longing, she added, 'All right, boy. You go to Papua New Guinea. But don't make promises about next summer. Otherwise I will be watching the road, and going down to the bus every day to see if you are on it.'

Tears began to mist my vision. I could just imagine my Nani walking down the road in summer with Kahu skipping beside her, and sitting on the verge watching the cars pass by, and asking the bus driver—

'We love you,' Nani said.

Waiting and waiting. Then the phone clicked and she was gone.

Eleven

I was two years with Jeff in Papua New Guinea and while they were productive years, they were not always happy. Jeff's father couldn't come down to Port Moresby to meet us but his mother, Clara, did. Although Jeff had told her I was a Maori it was obvious that I was still too dark. As soon as I stepped off the plane I could almost hear her wondering, 'Oh, my goodness, how am I going to explain this to the women at the Bridge Club?' But she was polite and gracious and kept up a lively chatter on the plane to Mount Hagen.

Tom, Jeff's father, was another story, and I liked him from the start. He was a self-made man whose confidence had not been shattered by his long and debilitating illness. But it was clear that he needed his son to help him. I can still remember the first time I saw Tom. He was standing on the verandah of the homestead, resting his weight on two crutches. He wasn't embarrassed by his disability and when Jeff went up to greet him he simply said, 'Gidday young fella. Glad to have you home.'

Tom had contracted Parkinson's disease. It wasn't until weeks later that I discovered the disease had not only struck at his limbs but also had rendered him partially blind.

The situation was clear. Jeff would have to act as an extension to his father, his arms and legs and eyes. Deskbound, Tom would run the plantation from the homestead and Jeff would translate the instructions into action. As for me, I've always been pretty good at hard work, so it was simply a matter of spitting on my hands and getting down to business.

Putting the plantation back on its feet was a challenge which the countryside really threw at us; I have never known a country which has fought back as hard as Papua New Guinea. I doubt if it can ever be tamed of its soaring temperatures, its terrain so much a crucible of crusted plateaus and valleys and its tribalism. But we tried, and I think we won some respite from the land, even if only for a short time. Man might carve his mark on the earth but unless he's vigilant, Nature will take it all back.

Sometimes, when you yourself are living life to the full, you forget that life elsewhere also continues to change like a chameleon. For instance, I used to marvel at the nationalism sweeping Papua New Guinea and the attempts by the Government to transplant national identity and customs onto the colonial face of the land. They were doing so despite an amazing set of difficulties: first, Papua New Guinea was fractionalised into hundreds of tribal groups with a thousand different tongues; second, there were so many outside influences on Papua New Guinea's inheritance, including their neighbours across the border in Irian Jaya; and, third, the new technology demanded that the people had to live 'one thousand years in one lifetime', from loincloth to the three-piece suit and computer knowledge in a simple step.

In many respects the parallels with the Maori in New Zealand were very close, except that we didn't have to advance as many years in one lifetime. However, our journey was possibly more difficult because it had to be undertaken within European terms of acceptability. We were a minority and much of our progress was dependent on European goodwill. And there was no doubt that in New Zealand, just as in Papua New Guinea, our nationalism was also galvanising the people to become one Maori nation.

So it was that in Australia and Papua New Guinea I grew into an understanding of myself as a Maori and, I guess, was being prepared for my date with destiny. Whether it had anything to do with Kahu's destiny, I don't know, but just as I was maturing in my own understanding she, too, was moving closer and closer to that point where she was in the right place, at the right time, with the right understanding to accomplish the task which had been assigned to her. In this respect there is no doubt in my mind that she had always been the *right* person.

My brother Porourangi has always been a good letter writer and he kept me in touch with the affairs of the people at home. I could tell that his chiefly prestige was growing, as was his spirit, and I appreciated his kindness in letting me know that although I was far from the family I was not forgotten. Apparently Koro Apirana had now begun a second series of schools for the young people of the Coast. Our Koro had accepted that Porourangi would be 'the one' in our generation to carry on the leadership of the people, but he was still looking for 'the one' in the present generation. 'He wants to find a young boy,' Porourangi jested, 'to pull the sword out of the stone, someone who has been marked by the Gods for the task. Nobody has so far been able to satisfy him.' Then, in one of his letters, Porourangi made my heart leap with joy. Ana had told him it was about time that Kahu came back to stay in Whangara, with her and Porourangi.

Kahu was then six years old; Rehua's mother had agreed and so Kahu returned. 'Well,' Porourangi wrote, 'you should have seen us all crying at the bus stop. Kahu got off the bus and she has grown so much, you wouldn't recognise her. Her first question, after all the hugging, was "Where's Paka? Is Paka here?" Nani Flowers said he was fishing, so she waited and waited all day down at the beach for him. When he came in, she leapt into his arms. But you know our Koro, as gruff as usual. Still, it is really good to have Kahu home.'

In his later letters Porourangi wrote about the problems he felt were facing the Maori people. He had gone with Koro Apirana to Raukawa country and had been very impressed with the way in which Raukawa was organising its youth resources to be in a position to help the people in the twenty-first century. 'Will *we* be ready?' he asked. 'Will we have prepared the people to cope with the new challenges and the new technology? And will they still be Maori?' I could tell that the last question was weighing heavily on his mind. In this respect we both recognised that the answer lay in Koro Apirana's persistence with the school sessions, for he was one of the very few who could pass on the sacred knowledge. Our Koro was like an old whale stranded in an alien present, but that was how it was supposed to be because he also had his role in the pattern of things, in the tides of the future.

Near the middle of our second year in Papua New Guinea Jeff and I could afford to relax a little. We took trips to Manus Island and it was there that Jeff put into words the thoughts that had been on my mind for some months.

'You're getting homesick, aren't you, Rawiri?' he said.

We had been diving in the lagoon, and in that wondrous blue water I had picked up a shining silver shell from the reef. I had taken it back to the beach and was listening to the sea whispering to me from the shell's silver whorls.

'A little,' I replied. Many things were coming to a head for me on the plantation, and I wanted to avoid a collision. Jeff and I were getting along okay but his parents were pushing him ever so gently to consort with his own kind in the clubs and all the parties of the aggressively expatriate. On my part, this had thrown me more into the company of the 'natives', like Bernard (who had more degrees than Clara had chins) and Joshua, who both worked on the farm. In so doing I had broken a cardinal rule and my punishment was ostracism.

'We've come a long way together,' Jeff said.

'We sure have,' I laughed. 'And there's still a way to go yet.'

Then Jeff said, 'I want to thank you. For everything. But if you have to go, I'll understand.'

I smiled at him, reflectively. I placed the shell back to my ear. *Hoki mai, hoki mai ki te wa kainga*, the sea whispered, *come home*.

Jeff and I returned to the plantation the next day. There was a letter waiting from Porourangi. Ana was expecting a baby, and the whole family was hoping that the child would be a son. 'Of all of us,' Porourangi wrote, 'Kahu seems to be the most excited. Koro Apirana, too, is over the moon.'

The letter had the effect of making me realise how much time had passed since I had been in the company of my people, my whanau. I felt a sudden keenness, like pincers squeezing my heart, to hold them all in my arms. *Hoki mai, hoki mai. Come home*.

Then three events occurred which convinced me that I should be homeward bound. The first happened when Jeff and his parents were invited to a reception hosted in Port Moresby for a young expatriate couple who'd just been wed. At first Clara's assumption was that I would stay back and look after the plantation, but Jeff said I was 'one of the family' and insisted I accompany them. Clara made it perfectly obvious that she was embarrassed by my presence and I was very saddened, at the reception, to hear her say to another guest, 'He's a friend of Jeff's. You know our Jeff, always bringing home dogs and strays. But at least he's not a native.' Her laughter glittered like knives.

But that was only a harbinger to the tragedy which took place when we returned to Mount Hagen. We had parked the station wagon at the airport and were driving home to the plantation. Jeff was at the wheel. We were all of us in a merry mood. The road was silver with moonlight. Suddenly, in front of us, I saw a man walking along the verge. I thought Jeff had seen him, too, and would move over to the middle of the road to pass him. But Jeff kept the station wagon pointed straight ahead.

The man turned. His arms came up, as if he was trying to defend himself. The front bumper crunched into his thighs and legs and he was catapulted into the windscreen which smashed into a thousand fragments. Jeff braked. The glass was suddenly splashed with blood. I saw a body being thrown ten metres to smash on the road. Clara screamed. Tom said, 'Oh, my God!' In the headlights and steam, the body moved.

I went to get out. Clara screamed again, 'Oh, no. No. His tribe could be on us any second. Payback, it could be payback for us. It's only a native.'

I pushed her away. Tom yelled, 'For God's sake, Rawiri, try to understand. You've heard the stories—'

I couldn't comprehend their fear. I looked at Jeff but he was just sitting there, stunned, staring at that broken body moving fitfully in the headlights. Then, suddenly, Jeff began to whimper. He started the motor.

'Let me out,' I hissed. 'Let me *out*. That's no native out there. That's *Bernard*.' A cous is a cous.

I yanked the door open. Clara yelled out to Jeff, 'Oh, I can see them.' Shadows on the road. 'Leave him here. Leave him.' Her words were high-pitched, frenzied. 'Oh. Oh. Oh.'

The station wagon careered past me. I will never forget Jeff's white face, so pallid, so fearful.

The second event occurred after the inquest. Bernard had died on the road that night. Who's to say that he would have lived had we taken him to hospital?

It was an accident, of course. A native walking carelessly on the side of the road. A cloud covering the moon for a moment. The native shouldn't have been there anyway. It could have happened to anybody.

'I don't blame you,' I said to Jeff. 'You can't help being who you are.' But all I could think of was the waste of a young man who had come one thousand years to his death on a moonlit road, the manner in which the earth must be mourning for one of its hopes and its sons in the new world, and the sadness that a friend I thought I had would so automatically react to the assumptions of his culture. *And would I be next?* There was nothing further to keep me here.

It was then that another letter came from Porourangi. The child, a girl, had been born. Naturally, Koro Apirana was disappointed and had blamed Nani Flowers again. In the same envelope was another letter, this one from Kahu.

'Dear Uncle Rawiri, how are you? We are well at Whangara. I have a baby sister. I like her very much. I am seven. Guess what, I am in the front row of our Maori culture group at school. I can do the poi. We are all lonesome for you. Don't forget me, will you. Love. Kahuia Te Rangi.'

Right at the bottom of Kahu's letter Nani Flowers had added just one word to express her irritation with my long absence from Whangara. *Bang.*

I flew out of Mount Hagen the following month. Jeff and I had a fond farewell, but already I could feel the strain between us. Clara was as polite and scintillating as usual. Tom was bluff and hearty.

'Good-bye, fella,' Tom said. 'You're always welcome.'

'Yes,' Jeff said. 'Always.' *Each to his own.*

The plane lifted into the air, Buffeted by the winds it finally stabilised and speared through the clouds.

Ah, yes, the clouds. The third event had been a strange cloud formation I had seen a month before above the mountains. The clouds looked like a surging sea and through them from far away a dark shape was approaching, slowly plunging. As it came closer and closer I saw that it was a giant whale. On its head was a sacred sign, a gleaming tattoo.

Haumi e, hui e, *taiki e.*

Let it be done.

Twelve

I wish I could say that I had a rapturous return. Instead, Nani Flowers growled at me for taking so long getting home, saying, 'I don't know why you wanted to go away in the first place. After all—'

'I know, Nani,' I said. 'There's nothing out there that I can't get here in Whangara.'

Bang came her hand. 'Don't *you* make fun of me, too,' she said, and she glared at Koro Apirana.

'Huh?' Koro said. 'I didn't say nothing.'

'But I can hear you *thinking*,' Nani Flowers said, 'and I know when you're funning me, you old paka.'

'Yeah, yeah, yeah,' Koro Apirana said. 'Te mea te mea.'

Before Nani Flowers could explode I gathered all of her in my arms (and there was much more of her now than there had been before) and kissed her. 'Well,' I said, 'I don't care if you're not glad to see me, because I'm glad to see *you*.'

Then I handed her the present I had bought her on my stopover in Sydney. You would have thought she'd be pleased but instead, *smack* came her hand again.

'You think you're smart, don't you,' she said.

I couldn't help it, but I had to laugh. 'Well how was I to know you'd put on weight!' My present had been a beautiful dress which was now three sizes too small.

That afternoon I was looking out the window when I saw Kahu running along the road. School had just finished.

I went to the verandah to watch her arrival. Was this the same little girl whose birth cord had been put in the earth those many years ago! Had seven years really gone past so quickly? I felt a lump at my throat. Then she saw me.

'Uncle Rawiri! she cried. 'You're back!'

The little baby had turned into a doe-eyed, long-legged beauty with a sparkle and infectious giggle in her voice. Her hair was unruly, but she had tamed it with hair clips. She was wearing a white dress and sandals. She ran up the steps and put her arms around my neck.

'Hullo,' she breathed as she gave me a kiss.

I held her tightly and closed my eyes. I hadn't realised how much I had missed the kid. Then Nani Flowers came out and said to Kahu, 'Enough of the loving. You and me are working girls! Come here! Be quick!'

'Nani and me are hoeing the vegetable garden,' Kahu smiled. 'I come every Wednesday to be her helper, when she wants a rest from Koro.' Then she gave a little gasp and took my hand and pulled me around to the shed at the back of the house.

'Don't be too long, Kahu,' Nani Flowers shouted. 'Those potatoes won't wait all day.'

Kahu waved okay. As I followed her I marvelled at the stream of conversation which poured out of her. 'I've got a baby sister now, uncle, she's a darling. Her name is Putiputi after Nani Flowers. Did you know I was top of my class this year? And I'm the leader of the culture group, too. I love singing the Maori songs. Will you teach me how to play the guitar? Oh, *neat*. And Daddy and Ana are coming to see you tonight once Daddy gets back from work. You bought me a *present? Me?* Oh where is it, where is it? You can show me later, eh. But I want you to see this first—'

She opened the door to the shed. Inside I saw a gleam of shining silver chrome. Kahu put her arms around me and kissed me again. It was my motorbike.

'Nani Flowers and I have been cleaning it every week,' she said. 'She used to cry sometimes, you know, when she was cleaning it. Then she'd get scared she might cause some rust.'

I just couldn't help it. I felt a rush of tears to my eyes. Concerned, Kahu stroked my face.

'Don't cry,' she said. 'Don't cry. It's all right, Uncle Rawiri. There, there. You're home now.'

Later that night Porourangi arrived. Among the family he was the one who seemed to have aged the most. He proudly showed me the new baby, Putiputi.

'Another girl,' Koro Apirana said audibly, but Porourangi took no notice of him. We were used to Koro's grumpy ways.

'Oh, be quiet,' Nani Flowers said. 'Girls can do anything these days. Haven't you heard you're not allowed to discriminate against women anymore?'

'I don't give a hang about women,' Koro Apirana said. 'You still haven't got the power.'

It was then that Nani Flowers surprised us all. 'Te mea te mea,' she said. 'Yeah, yeah, yeah, you old goat.'

We had a big family dinner that night with Maori bread and crayfish and lots of wine to drink. Nani had invited the boys over and they arrived with a roar and a rush of blue smoke and petrol fumes. It was almost as if I had never left. The guitars came out and the voices rang free. Nani Flowers was in her element, playing centre stage to her family, and one of the boys got her up to do a hula.

'Look,' he cried with delight. 'The Queen of Whangara!'

There was a roar of laughter at that one, and Kahu came running up to me, saying, 'See how we love you, uncle. We killed the fatted calf for you, just like the Bible says.' She hugged me close and then skipped away.

Then Porourangi was there. 'Is it good to be home?' he asked cautiously.

'Yes,' I breathed. 'Just *fantastic*. How has it been?'

'Much the same as ever,' Porourangi said. 'And you know our Koro. He's still looking.'

'What for?'

'The one who can pull the sword,' Porourangi laughed hollowly. 'There are a few more young boys he's found. One of them may be the one.'

Porourangi fell silent. I saw Koro Apirana rocking in his chair, back and forth, back and forth. Kahu came up to him and put her hand in his. He pushed her away and she dissolved into the dark. The guitars played on.

Over the following weeks it was clear to me that Koro Apirana's search for 'the one' had become an obsession. Ever since the birth of Kahu's sister he had become more intense and brooding. Perhaps aware of his own mortality, he wanted to make sure that the succession in the present generation was done – and done well. But in doing so he was pushing away the one who had always adored him, Kahu herself.

'You'd think the sun shone out of his—' Nani Flowers said rudely. Kahu had ridden a horse to the homestead that morning with the news that she'd come first in her Maori class. Nani Flowers had watched as Koro Apirana had dismissed the young girl. 'I don't know why she keeps on with him.'

'I know why,' I said to Nani Flowers. 'You remember when she bit his toe?' Even then she was telling him. "Yeah, don't think you're going to keep me out of this!"'

Nani Flowers shrugged her shoulders. 'Well, whatever it is, Kahu is sure a sucker for punishment, the poor kid. Must be my Muriwai breed. Or Mihi.'

Mihi Kotukutuku had been the mother of Ta Eruera, who had been Nani's cousin, and we loved the stories of Mihi's exploits. She was a big chief, descended as she was from Apanui, after whom Nani's tribe was named. The story we liked best was the one telling how Mihi had stood on sacred ground at Rotorua. 'Sit down,' a chief had yelled, enraged. 'Sit down,' because women weren't supposed to stand up and speak on sacred ground. But Mihi had replied,' 'No *you* sit down! I am a senior line to yours!' Not only that, but Mihi had then turned her back to him, bent over, lifted up her petticoats, and said, 'Anyway, here is the place where you come from!' That was Mihi's way of reminding the chief that all men are born of women.

We sat there on the verandah, talking about Kahu and how beautiful she was, both inside and outside. She had no guile. She had no envy. She had no jealousy. As we were talking, we saw Koro Apirana going down to the school where seven boys were waiting.

'Them's the contenders,' Nani Flowers said. 'One of them's going to be the Rocky of Whangara.'

Suddenly Kahu arrived, dawdling from the opposite direction. She looked so disconsolate and sad. Then she saw Koro Apirana. Her face lit up and she ran to him, crying 'Paka! Oh! Paka!'

He turned to her quickly. 'Go back,' he said. 'Go away. You are of no use to me.'

Kahu stopped in her tracks. I thought she would cry, but she knitted her eyebrows and gave him a look of such frustration that I could almost hear her saying to herself, 'You just wait, Paka, you just wait.' Then she skipped over to us as if nothing had happened.

I was lucky enough to get a job in town stacking timber in a timber yard and delivering orders to contractors on site. Every morning I'd beep the horn of my motorbike as I passed Porourangi's house, to remind Kahu it was time for her to get up for school. I soon began to stop and wait until I saw her head poking above the window sill to let me know she was awake. 'Thank you, Uncle Rawiri,' she would call as I roared off to work.

Sometimes after work I would find Kahu waiting at the highway for me. 'I came down to welcome you home,' she would explain. 'Nani doesn't want any help today. Can I have a ride on your bike? I *can*? Oh, *neat*.' She would clamber on behind me and hold on tight. As we negotiated the track to the village I would be swept away by her ingenuous chatter. 'Did you have a good day, uncle? I had a *neat* day except for maths, yuck, but if I want to go to university I have to learn things I don't like. Did you go to university, uncle? Koro says it's a waste of time for a girl to go. Sometimes I wish I wasn't a girl. Then Koro would love me more than he does. But I don't mind. What's it like being a boy, uncle? Have you got a girlfriend? There's a boy at school who keeps following me around. I said to him that he should try Linda. She likes boys. As for me, I've only got one boyfriend. No, *two*. No, *three*. Koro, Daddy and *you*. Did you miss me in Australia, uncle? Did you like Papua New Guinea? Nani Flowers thought you'd end up in a pot over a fire. She's a hardcase, isn't she! You didn't forget me, uncle, did you? You didn't, eh? Well, thank you for the ride, Uncle Rawiri. See you tomorrow. Bye now.' With an ill-aimed kiss and a hug, and a whirl of white dress, she would be gone.

The end of the school year came, and the school break-up ceremony was to be held on a Friday evening. Kahu had sent invitations to the whole family and included the boys in the list. 'You are cordially invited,' the card read, 'to my school prizegiving and I do hope you are able to attend. No RSVP is required. Love, Kahutia Te Rangi. P.S. No leather jackets please, as this is a formal occasion. P.P.S. Please park all motorbikes in the area provided and not in the headmaster's parking space like last year. I do not wish to be embraced again.'

On the night of the break-up ceremony, Nani Flowers said to me, as she was getting dressed. 'What's this word "embraced"?'

'I think she means "embarrassed",' I said.

'Well, how do I look?' Nani asked.

She was feeling very pleased with herself. She had let out the dress I had bought her and added lime-green panels to the sides. Nani was colour blind and thought they were red. I gulped hard. 'You look like a duchess,' I lied.

'Not like a queen?' Nani asked, offended. 'Well, I'll soon fix that.' Oh no, not the *hat*. It must have looked wonderful in the 1930s but that was ages ago. Ever since, she had added a bit of this and a bit of that until it looked just like something out of her vegetable garden.

'Oh,' I swallowed, 'you look out of this world.'

She giggled coyly. We made our way out to Porourangi's car. Kahu's face gleamed out at us.

'Oh, you look lovely,' she said to Nani, 'but there's something wrong with your hat.' She made a space for Nani and said to her, 'Come and sit by me, darling, and I'll fix it for you.'

Porourangi whispered to me, 'Couldn't you stop the old lady? Her and her blinking hat.'

I was laughing too hard to answer. In the back seat Kahu was adding some feathers and flowers and what looked like weeds. The strange thing was that in fact the additions made the hat just right.

The school hall was crowded. Kahu took us to our places and sat us down. There was an empty seat beside Nani with 'Reserved' on it.

'That's for Koro when he comes,' she said. 'And don't the boys look *neat*?' At the back of the hall the boys were trying to hide behind their suit jackets.

Nani Flowers jabbed Porourangi in the ribs. 'Didn't you tell that kid?' she asked.

'I didn't have the heart,' he whispered.

For the rest of that evening the seat beside Nani Flowers remained empty, like a gap in a row of teeth. Kahu seemed to be in everything – the school choir, the

67

skits, the gymnastics. After every item she would skip back to us and say, 'Isn't Koro here yet? He's missing the best part.'

Then the second half of the programme began. There was Kahu in her skirt and bodice, standing so proudly in front of the school cultural group. 'Hands on hips!' she yelled. 'Let's begin!' she ordered. And as she sang, she smiled a brilliant smile at all of us. Her voice rang out with pride.

'That young girl's a cracker,' I overheard someone say. But my heart was aching for her and I wanted to leave. Nani Flowers gripped me hard and said, 'No, we all have to sit here, like it or not.' Her lips were quivering.

The performances continued, one after another, and I could see that Kahu had realised that Koro Apirana was not going to arrive. The light kept dimming, gradually fading from her face, like a light bulb flickering. By the time the cultural group was finished, she was staring down at the floor trying not to see us. She looked as if she was feeling ashamed, and I loved her all the more for her vulnerability.

We tried to bolster her courage by clapping loudly, and we were rewarded by a tremulous smile playing on her face. It was then that the headmaster stepped forward. He made an announcement: one of the students would read the speech which had won the East Coast primary schools contest. What was remarkable, he said, was that the student had given it entirely in her own tongue, the Maori language. He called for Kahutia Te Rangi to come forward.

'Did you know about this?' Nani Flowers asked.

'No,' said Porourangi. 'Come to think of it, she did mention she had a surprise. For her Koro—'

To the cheers of her classmates Kahu advanced to the front of the stage.

'E nga rangatira,' Kahu began, 'e nga iwi,' she looked at Koro Apirana's empty seat, 'tena koutou, tena koutou, tena koutou katoa.' There were stars in her eyes, like sparkling tears. 'Distinguished guests, members of the audience, my speech is a speech of love for my great-grandfather, Koro Apirana.'

Nani Flowers gave a sob, and tears began to flow down her cheeks.

Kahu's voice was cler and warm as she told of her love for her great-grandfather and her respect for him. He tones rang with pride as she recited our genealogy, the family whakapapa. She conveyed how grateful she was to live in Whangara and that her main aim in life was to fulfil the wishes of her great-grandfather and of the tribe.

And I felt so proud of her, so proud, and so sad that Koro Apirana was not there to hear how much she loved him. And I wanted to shout, *Well done, good for you*, to this young girl who was not really so brave and who would have liked the support of the one person who was never there – her Koro. At the end of the speech I leapt to my feet to do a haka of support for her. Then the boys were joining in, and Nani Flowers was kicking off her shoes. The sadness and the joy swept us all away in acknowledging Kahu, but we knew that her heart was aching for Koro Apirana.

In the car, later, Porourangi said, 'Your Koro couldn't make it tonight, darling.'

'That's all right, daddy. I don't mind.'

Nani Flowers hugged her fiercely. 'I tell you, Kahu, tomorrow I'm really getting a divorce. Your Koro can go his way and I'll go mine.'

Kahu put her face against Nani Flowers' cheeks. Her voice was drained and defeated. 'It's not Paka's fault, Nani,' she said, 'that I'm a girl.'

Thirteen

Two weeks after the school break-up ceremony, Koro Apirana took the young boys from the school onto the sea. It was early morning as he put them in his boat and headed out past the bay where the water suddenly turned dark green.

When the sun tipped the sea, Koro Apirana began a prayer. He had a carved stone in his hand and suddenly he threw it into the ocean. The boys watched until they could see it no longer.

'One of you must bring that stone back to me,' Koro Apirana said. 'Go now.'

The boys were eager to prove themselves, but the stone had gone too deep. Some were afraid of the darkness. Others were unable to dive so far down. Despite valiant attempts they could not do it.

Koro Apirana's face sagged. 'Okay, boys, you've done well. Let's get you all home.'

When he got back home, Koro Apirana shut himself in the bedroom. Slowly, he began to lament.

'What's wrong with my Koro?' Kahu asked. She was sitting with me on the verandah. 'Is it because of the stone?'

'How did you know about that?' I asked, astonished.

'One of the boys told me,' Kahu said. 'I wish I could make Paka happy again.' Her eyes held a hint of gravity.

The next morning I was up early, intending to go out onto the sea in my dinghy. To my surprise, Kahu was waiting at the door in her white dress and sandals. There were white ribbons in her pigtails.

'Can I come for a ride in your boat, Uncle Rawiri?' she asked.

I couldn't really say say no, so I nodded my head. Just as we were ready to leave, Nani Flowers yelled out, '*Hoi*, wait for me!' She had decided to join us. 'I can't stand to hear the old paka feeling sorry for himself. Mmmm, what a beautiful day! The sun is shining.'

We rowed out past the bay and Kahu asked again about the stone.

'What stone!' Nani Flowers said.

So I told her, and Nani wanted to be shown where it had been dropped into the water. We went out into the ocean where it suddenly turned indigo.

'Goodness,' Nani said. 'No wonder those boys couldn't get it. This is *deep*.'

'Does Koro Apirana really want it back?' Kahu asked.

'Yeah, I suppose he must,' Nani Flowers said, 'the old paka. Well, serve him right for—'

Kahu said simply, 'I'll get it.'

Before we could stop her she stood up and dived overboard. Until that moment I had never even known she could swim.

Nani's mouth made a big 'O'. Then the breath rushed into her lungs and she screamed, 'Oh, no!' She jabbed me hard and said, 'Go after her, Rawiri, *Go*.' She virtually pushed me over the side of the rowboat.

'Give me the diving mask,' I yelled. Nani Flowers threw it at me and quickly I put it on. I took three deep breaths and did a duck dive.

I couldn't see her. The sea looked empty. There was only a small stingray flapping down towards the reef.

Then I got a big fright because the stingray turned around and, smiling, waved at me. It was Kahu in her white dress and sandals, dog paddling down to the sea floor, her braids floating around her head.

I gasped and swallowed sea water. I came to the surface coughing and spluttering.

'Where is she!' Nani Flowers screamed. 'Has she drowned? Oh, no, my Kahu.' And before I could stop her she jumped in beside me, just about emptying the whole ocean. She didn't even give me a chance to explain as she grabbed the mask off me and put it on. Then she tried to swim underwater, but her dress was so filled with air that no matter how hard she tried she remained on the surface like a balloon with legs kicking out of it. I doubt if she could have gotten deeper anyway because she was so fat she couldn't sink.

'Oh, Kahu,' Nani Flowers cried again. But this time I told her to take a deep breath and, when she was looking underwater, to watch where I would point.

We went beneath the surface. Suddenly I pointed down. Kahu was searching the reef, drifting around the coral. Nani Flowers' eyes widened with disbelief.

Whatever it was Kahu was searching for, she was having difficulty finding it. But just then white shapes came speeding out of the dark towards her. I thought they were sharks, and Nani Flowers began to blow bubbles of terror.

They were dolphins. They circled around Kahu and seemed to be talking to her. She nodded and grabbed one around its body. As quick as a flash, the dolphins sped her to another area of the reef and stopped. Kahu seemed to say, 'Down here?' and the dolphins made a nodding motion.

Suddenly Kahu made a quick, darting gesture. She picked something up, inspected it, appeared satisfied with it, and went back to the dolphins. Slowly the girl and the dolphins rose towards us. But just as they were midway, Kahu stopped again. She kissed the dolphins goodbye and gave Nani Flowers a heart attack by returning to the reef. She picked up a crayfish and resumed her upward journey. The dolphins were like silver dreams as they disappeared.

Nani Flowers and I were treading water when Kahu appeared between us, smoothing her hair back from her face and blinking away the sea water. Nani Flowers, sobbing, hugged her close in the water.

'I'm all right, Nani,' Kahu laughed.

She showed the crayfish to us. 'This is for Paka's tea,' she said. 'And you can give him back his stone.'

She placed the stone in Nani Flowers' hands.

Nani Flowers looked at me quickly. As we were pulling ourselves back into the dinghy she said, 'Not a word about this to Koro Apirana.'

I nodded. I looked back landward and in the distance saw the carving of Paikea on his whale like a portent.

As we got to the beach, Nani Flowers said again, 'Not a word, Rawiri. Not a word about the stone or our Kahu.' She looked up at Paikea.

'He's not ready yet,' she said.

The sea seemed to be trembling with anticipation.

Haumi e, hui e, *taiki e*.

Let it be done.

Winter

Whale Song,
Whale Rider

Fourteen

The muted thunder boomed under water like a great door opening far away. Suddenly the sea was filled with awesome singing, a song with eternity in it. Then the whale burst through the sea and astride the head was a man. He was wondrous to look upon. He was the whale rider.

He had come, the whale rider, from the sacred island far to the east. He had called to the whale, saying, 'Friend, you and I must take the gifts of life to the new land, life-giving seeds to make it fruitful.' The journey had been long and arduous, but the whale had been filled with joy at the close companionship they shared as they sped through the southern seas.

Then they had arrived at the land, and at a place called Whangara the golden rider had dismounted. He had taken the gifts of Hawaiki to the people and the land and sea had blossomed.

For a time the whale had rested in the sea which sighed at Whangara. Time had passed like a swift current, but in its passing had come the first tastes of separation. His golden master had met a woman and had married her. Time passed, time passed like a dream. One day, the whale's golden master had come to the great beast and there had been sadness in his eyes.

'One last ride, friend,' his master had said.

In elation, anger and despair, the whale had taken his golden master deeper than ever before and had sung to him of the sacred islands and of their friendship. But his master had been firm. At the end of the ride, he had said,

'I have been fruitful and soon children will come to me. My destiny lies here. As for you, return to the Kingdom of Tangaroa and to your own kind.'

The heartache of that separation had never left the whale, nor had the remembrance of that touch of brow to brow in the last hongi.

Antarctica. The Well of the World. Te Wai Ora o te Ao. Above, the frozen continent was swept with an inhuman, raging storm. Below, where the Furies could not reach, the sea was calm and unworldly. The light played gently on the frozen ice layer and bathed the undersea kingdom with an unearthly radiance. The giant roots of the ice extending down from the surface sparkled, glowed, twinkled and flashed prisms of light like strobes in a vast subterranean cathedral. The ice cracked, moaned, shivered and susurrated with rippling glissandi, a giant organ playing a titanic symphony.

Within the fluted ice chambers the herd of whales moved with infinite grace in holy procession. As they did so they offered their own choral harmony to the natural orchestration. Their movements were languid and lyrical, and belied the physical reality of their sizes; their tail flukes gently stroked the water, manoeuvring them ever southward. Around and above them the sealions, penguins and other Antarctic denizens darted, circled and swooped in graceful waltz.

Then the whales could go no further. Their sonics indicated that there was nothing in front except a solid wall of ice. Bewildered, the ancient bull whale let loose a ripple of harmonics, a plaintive cry for advice. Had his golden master been with him, he would have been given the direction in which to turn.

All of a sudden a shaft of light penetrated the underwater world and turned it into a gigantic hall of mirrors. In each one the ancient whale seemed to see a vision of himself being spurred ahead by his golden master. He made a quick turn and suddenly shards of ice began to cascade like spears around the herd. The elderly females throbbed their alarm to him. They were already further south than they had ever been before and the mirrors, for them, appeared only to reflect a crystal tomb for the herd. They communicated the urgency of the situation to their leader.

The aurora australis played above the ice world and the reflected light was like a mesmerising dream to the ancient bull whale. He began to follow the light, turning away from the southward plunge. As he did so he increased his speed, and the turbulence of his wake caused ice waterfalls within the undersea kingdom.Twenty metres long, he no longer possessed the flexibility to manoeuvre at speed.

The herd followed through the crashing, falling ice. They saw their leader rising to the surface and watched as the surface starred around him. They began to mourn, for they knew that their journey to the dangerous islands was now a reality. Their leader was totally ensnared in the rhapsody of his dreams of the golden rider. So long part of their own whakapapa and legend, the golden rider could not be dislodged from their leader's thoughts. The last journey had begun and at the end of it Death was waiting.

The aurora australis was like Hine Nui Te Po, Goddess of Death, flashing above the radiant land. The whales swept swiftly through the southern seas.

Haumi e, hui e, taiki e.

Let it be done.

Fifteen

Not long after Kahu's dive for the stone, in the early hours of the morning, a young man was jogging along Wainui Beach, not far from Whangara, when he noticed a great disturbance on the sea. 'The horizon all of a sudden got lumpy,' he said as he tried to describe the phenomenon, 'and lumps were moving in a solid mass to the beach.' As he watched, the jogger realised that he was witnessing the advance to the beach of a great herd of whales. 'They kept coming and coming,' he told the *Gisborne Herald*, 'and they did not turn away. I ran down to the breakwater. All around me the whales were stranding themselves. They were whistling, an eerie, haunting sound. Every now and then they would spout. I felt like crying.'

The news was quickly communicated to the town, and the local radio and television stations sent reporters out to Wainui. One enterprising cameraman hired a local helicopter to fly him over the scene. It is his flickering film images that most of us remember. In the early morning light, along three kilometres of coastland, are two hundred whales – male, female, young – waiting to die. The waves break over them and hiss around their passive frames. Dotted on the beach are human shapes, drawn to the tragedy. The pilot of the helicopter says on camera, 'I've been to Vietnam, y'know, and I've done deer culling down south.' His lips are trembling and his eyes are moist with tears. 'But I swear, this is like seeing the end of the world.'

One particular sequence of the news film will remain indelibly imprinted on our minds. The camera zooms in on one of the whales, lifted high onto the beach by the waves. A truck has been driven down beside the whale. The whale is on its side, and blood is streaming from its mouth. The whale is still alive.

Five men are working on the whale. They are splattered with blood. As the helicopter hovers above them, one of the men stops his work and smiles directly into the camera. The look is triumphant. He lifts his arms in a victory sign and the camera focuses on the other men, where they stand in the surging water. The chainsaw has just completed cutting through the whale's lower jaw. The men are laughing as they wrench the jaw from the butchered whale. There is a huge spout of blood as the jaw suddenly snaps free. The blood drenches the men in a dark gouting stream. Blood, laughing, pain, victory, blood.

It was that sequence of human butchery, more than any other, which triggered feelings of sorrow and anger among the people on the Coast. Some would have argued that in Maori terms a stranded whale was traditionally a gift from the Gods and that the actions could therefore be condoned. But others felt more primal feelings of love for the beasts which had once been our companions from the Kingdom of the Lord Tangaroa. Nor was this just a question of one whale among many; this was a matter of two hundred members of a vanishing species.

At the time Kahu had just turned eight and Koro Apirana was down in the South Island with Porourangi. I rang them up to tell them what was happening. Koro said, 'Yes, we know. Porourangi has rung the airport to see if we can get on the plane. But the weather's bad and we can't get out. You'll have to go to Wainui. This is a sign to us. I don't like it. I don't like it at all.'

Knowing Kahu's kinship with the sea, I was glad that she had still been asleep when the news was broadcast.

I said to Nani Flowers, 'You better keep our Kahu at home today. Don't let her know what has happened.' Nani's eyes glistened. She nodded her head.

I got on my motorbike and went round rousing the boys. I hadn't realised it before, but when you catch people unawares you sure find out a lot about them. For instance, one of the boys slept on his stomach with his thumb in his mouth. Billy had his hair in curlers and a cigarette dangling from his lips. And a third slept with all his clothes on and the motorbike was beside the bed in his bedroom.

'Come on, boys,' I said. 'We've got work to do.' We assembled at the crossroads, gunned our bikes, and then took off. Instead of going the long way by road we cut across country and beach, flying like spears to help save the whales. The wind whistled among us as we sped over the landscape. Billy led the way and we followed – he was sure tricky, all right, knowing the shortcuts. No wonder the cops could never catch him. We flew over fences, jounced around paddocks, leapt streams, and skirted the incoming tide. We were all whooping and hollering with the excitement of the ride when Billy took us up to a high point overlooking Wainui.

'There they are,' he said.

Gulls were wheeling above the beach. For as far as the eye could see whales were threshing in the curve of sand. The breakers were already red with blood. We sped down on our rescue mission.

The gulls cried, outraged, as we roared through their gathering numbers. The first sight to greet our eyes was this old European lady who had sat down on a whale that some men were pulling onto the beach with a tractor. They had put a rope round the whale's rear flukes and were getting angrier and angrier with the woman, manhandling her away. But she would just return and sit on the whale again, her eyes determined. We came to the rescue and that was the first fistfight of the day.

'Thank you, gentlemen,' the lady said. 'The whale is already dead of course, but how can men be so venal?'

By that time many of the locals were out on the beach. Some of them still had their pyjamas on. There were a lot of elderly people living near Wainui and it was amazing to see them trying to stop younger men from pillaging the whales. When one of the old women saw us, she set her mouth grimly and raised a pink slipper in a threatening way.

'Hey lady,' Billy said. 'We're the good guys.'

She gaped disbelievingly. Then she said, 'Well, if you're the good guys, you'd better go after them bad guys.' She pointed down to where a truck was parked beside a dying whale. There were several beefy guys loading a dismembered jaw onto the back. As we approached we saw an old man scuffling with them. One of the young men smacked him in the mouth and the old man went down. His wife gave a high-pitched scream.

We roared up to the truck.

'Hey, *man*,' I hissed. 'That whale belongs to Tangaroa.' I pointed to the dying beast. The stench of guts and blood was nauseous. Seagulls dived into the bloodied surf.

'Who's stopping us?'

'We are,' Billy said. He grabbed the chainsaw, started it up and, next minute, had sawn the front tyres of the truck. That started the second fistfight of the day.

It was at this stage that the police and rangers arrived. I guess they must have had trouble figuring out who were the good guys and who were the bad guys because they started to manhandle us as well. Then the old lady with the pink slipper arrived. She waved it in front of the ranger and said, 'Not *them*, you stupid fool. They're on *our* side.'

The ranger laughed. He looked us over quickly. 'In that case, lady, I guess we'll have to work together. Okay, fellas?'

I looked at the boys. We had a strange relationship with the cops. But this time we nodded agreement.

'Okay,' the ranger said. 'The name's Derek. Let's get this beach cleared and cordoned off. We've got some Navy men coming in soon from Auckland.' He yelled, 'Anybody here got wet suits? If so, get into them. We'll need all the help we can get.'

The boys and I cleared the beach. We mounted a bike patrol back and forth along the sand, keeping the spectators back from the water. The locals helped us. I saw a shape I thought I knew tottering down to the sea. The woman must have borrowed her son's wet suit, but I would have recognised those pink slippers anywhere.

All of us who were there that day and night will be forever bonded by our experience with the stranded whales. They were tightly bunched and they were crying like babies. Derek had assigned people in groups, eight people to look after each whale. 'Try to keep them cool,' he said. 'Pour water over them, otherwise they'll dehydrate. The sun's going to get stronger. Keep pouring that water, but try to keep their blowholes clear – otherwise they'll suffocate. Above all, try to stop them from lying on their sides.'

It was difficult and heavy work, and I marvelled at the strength that some of the elderly folk brought to the task. One of the old men was talking to his whale and said in response to his neighbour, 'Well, *you* talk to your plants!' At that point the whale lifted its head and, staring at the two men, gave what appeared to be a giggle. 'Why, the whale understands,' the old man said. So the word went down the line of helpers.

> *Talk to the whales*
> *They understand.*
> *They understand.*

The tide was still coming in. The Navy personnel arrived and members of Greenpeace, Project Jonah, and

Friends of the Earth, also. Two helicopters whirred overhead, dropping wetsuited men into the sea.

A quick conference was called on the situation. The decision was made to try and tow the whales out to sea. Small runabouts were used, and while most of the whales resisted being towed, there were some successes. In that first attempt, a hundred and forty whales were refloated. There were many cheers along the beach. But the whales were like confused children, milling and jostling out in the deeper water, and they kept trying to return to those who were still stranded along the beach, darting back to those who were already dead. The cheers became ragged when all the whales returned to beach themselves again at low tide.

'Okay, folks,' Derek called. 'We're back at the beginning. Let's keep them cool. And let's keep our spirits up.'

The sea thundered through his words. The seagulls screamed overhead. The sun reached noon and began its low decline. I saw children coming from buses to help. Some schools had allowed senior students to aid the rescue. Many of the old folk were pleased to be relieved. Others, however, stayed on. For them, *their* whale had become a member of the family. 'And I can't leave Sophie now,' an elderly lady said. The sun scattered its spokes across the sand.

The whales kept dying. As each death occurred the people who were looking after the whale would weep and clasp one another. They would try to force away the younger, healthier whales which had returned to keep company with their dying mates. When a large whale was turning on its side, several juveniles would try to assist it, rubbing their bodies against the dying whale's head. All the time the animals were uttering cries of distress or alarm, like lost children.

Some old people refused to leave the beach. They began to sing 'Onward Christian Soldiers'. They continued to try to right the whales, rocking them back and forth to restore their balance, and encouraging them to swim in groups. It was soon obvious, however, that the whales did not wish to be separated. So the ranger decided that an effort should be made to herd the surviving whales as one large group out to sea. They seemed to sense that we were trying to help them and offered no resistance or harm. When we reached them, most were exhausted, but when they felt us lifting them up and pushing them out to sea they put their energy into swimming and blowing.

Somehow we managed to get the whales out again with the incoming tide. But all they did was to cry and grieve for their dead companions; after wallowing aimlessly, they would return to nuzzle their loved ones. The sea hissed and fell, surged and soughed upon the sand. The whales were singing a plaintive song, a fluting sound which began to recede away, away, away.

By evening, all the whales had died. Two hundred whales, lifeless on the beach and in the water. The boys and I waited during the death throes. Some of the people from the town had set up refreshments and were serving coffee. I saw the lady with the pink slippers sipping coffee and looking out to sea.

'Remember me?' I said. 'My name's Rawiri. I'm a good guy.'

There were tears in her eyes. She pressed my hand in companionship.

'Even the good guys,' she said, 'can't win all the time.'

When I returned to Whangara that night, Nani Flowers said, 'Kahu knows about the whales.' I found Kahu way up on the bluff, calling out to sea. She was making that mewling sound and then cocking her head to listen for a reply. The sea was silent, eternal.

I comforted her. The moon was drenching the sky with loneliness. I heard an echo of Koro Apirana's voice, 'This is a sign to us. I don't like it.' Suddenly with great clarity, I knew that our final challenge was almost upon us. I pressed Kahu close to me, to reassure her. I felt a sudden shiver as far out to sea, muted thunder boomed like a door opening far away.

Haumi e, hui e, *taiki e*.

Let it be done.

Sixteen

Yes, people in the district vividly remember the stranding of the whales because television and radio brought the event into our homes that evening. But there were no television cameras or radio newsmen to see what occurred in Whangara the following night. Perhaps it was just as well, because even now it all seems like a dream. Perhaps, also, the drama enacted that night was only meant to be seen by the tribe and nobody else. Whatever the case, the earlier stranding of whales was merely a prelude to the awesome event that followed, an event that had all the cataclysmic power and grandeur of a Second Coming.

The muted thunder and forked lightning the day before had advanced quickly across the sea like an illuminated cloud. We saw it as a great broiling rush of the elements; with it came the icy cold winds hurled from the Antarctic.

Nani Flowers, Kahu and I were watching the weather anxiously. We were at the airport, waiting for the flight bringing Koro Apirana and Porourangi back to us. Suddenly there was the plane, bucking like an albatross, winging ahead of winds which heralded the arrival of the storm. It was as if Tawhirimatea was trying to smash the plane down to earth in anger.

Koro Apirana was pale and upset. He and Nani Flowers were always arguing, but this time he was genuinely relieved to see her. 'Oh, wife,' he whispered as he held her tightly.

'We had a hard time down South,' Porourangi said, trying to explain Koro's agitation. 'The land dispute was a difficult one and I think that Koro is worried about the judge's decision. Then when he heard about the whales, he grew very sombre.'

The wind began to whistle and shriek like wraiths.

'Something's going on,' Koro Apirana whispered. 'I don't know what it is. But something—'

'It's all right,' Kahu soothed. 'It will be all right, Paka.'

We collected the suitcases and ran out to the station wagon. As we drove through the town the illuminated cloud seemed always to be in front of us, like a portent.

Even before we reached Wainui Beach we could smell and taste the Goddess of Death. The wind was still lashing like a whip at the landscape. The car was buffeted strongly, and Nani Flowers was holding on to her seat belt nervously.

'It's all right,' Kahu said. 'There, there, Nani.'

Suddenly, in front of the car, I could see a traffic officer waving his torch. He told us to drive carefully as earth-moving machinery was digging huge trenches in the sand for the dead whales. Then he recognised me as one of the people who had tried to help. His smile and salute were sad.

I drove carefully along the highway. On our right I could see the hulking shapes of the graders, silhouetted against the broiling sky. Further down the beach, at the ocean's edge, were the whales, rocked by the surge and hiss of the sea. The whole scene was like a surreal painting, not nightmarish, but immensely tragic. What had possessed the herd to be so suicidal? The wind hurled sand and mud at the windscreen of the station wagon. We watched in silence.

Then, 'Stop,' Koro Apirana said.

I stopped the station wagon. Koro Apirana got out. He staggered against the onslaught of the wind.

'Leave him,' Nani Flowers said. 'Let him be with the whales by himself. He needs to mourn.'

But I was fearful of Koro's distraught state. I got out of the car, too. The wind was freezing. I walked over to him. His eyes were haunted. He looked at me, uncomprehending.

'No wai te he?' he shouted. 'Where lies the blame?'

And the seagulls caught his words within their claws and screamed and echoed the syllables overhead.

When we turned back to the station wagon I saw Kahu's white face, so still against the window.

'This is a sign to us,' Koro Apirana said again.

We turned off the main highway and onto the road to Whangara. It was so dark that I switched the headlights on full. I looked up at that illuminated cloud. I had the strangest feeling that its centre was just above the village. I felt a rush of fear and was very glad when Whangara came into sight.

Whangara must be one of the most beautiful places in the world, like a kingfisher's nest floating on the water at summer solstice. There it was, with church in the foreground and marae behind, silhouetted against the turbulent sea. And there was Paikea, our eternal sentinel, always vigilant against any who would wish to harm his descendants. Caught like this, the village was a picture of normality given the events that were to come.

I drove up to the house.

'Kahu, you help take Koro's bags inside,' I said. 'Then I'll take you and Daddy home. Okay?'

Kahu nodded. She put her arms around her great-grandfather and said again, 'It's all right, Paka. Everything will be all right.'

She picked up a small flight bag and carried it up onto the verandah. We were all getting out of the wagon and climbing towards her when, suddenly, the wind died away.

I will never forget the look on Kahu's face. She was gazing out to sea and it was as if she was looking back into the past. It was a look of calm, of acceptance. It forced us all to turn to see what Kahu was seeing.

The land sloped away to the sea. The surface of the water was brilliant green, blending into dark blue and then a rich purple. The illuminated cloud was seething above one place on the horizon.

All of a sudden there was a dull booming from beneath the water, like a giant door opening a thousand years ago. At the place below the clouds the surface of the sea shimmered like gold dust. Then streaks of blue lightning came shooting out of the sea like missiles. I thought I saw something flying through the air, across the aeons, to plunge into the heart of the village.

A dark shadow began to ascend from the deep. Then there were other shadows rising, ever rising. Suddenly the first shadow breached the surface and I saw it was a whale. Leviathan. Climbing through the depths. Crashing through the skin of sea. And as it came, the air was filled with streaked lightning and awesome singing.

Koro Apirana gave a tragic cry, for this was no ordinary beast, no ordinary whale. This whale came from the past. As it came it filled the air with its singing.

Karanga mai, karanga mai,
karanga mai.

Its companions began to breach the surface also, orchestrating the call with unearthly music.

The storm finally unleashed its fury and strength upon the land. The sea was filled with whales and in their vanguard was their ancient battle-scarred leader.

Karanga mai, karanga mai,
karanga mai.

On the head of the whale was the sacred sign. A swirling tattoo, flashing its power across the darkening sky.

I zoomed on my bike through the night and the rain, rounding the boys up. 'I'm sorry, boys,' I said to them as I yanked them out of bed, 'we're needed again.'

'Not more whales,' they groaned.

'Yes,' I said. 'But this is different, boys, different. These whales are right here in Whangara.'

Koro Apirana had issued his instructions to Porourangi and me. We were to gather up the boys and all the available men of the village, and tell them to come to the meeting house. And we were to hurry.

'Huh?' Nani Flowers had said in a huff. 'What about us women! We've got hands to help.'

Koro Apirana smiled a wan smile. His voice was firm as he told her, 'I don't want you to interfere, Flowers. You know as well as I do that this is sacred work.'

Nani Flowers bristled. 'But you haven't got enough men to help. You watch out. If I think you need the help, well, I shall change myself into a man. Just like Muriwai.'

'In the meantime,' Koro Apirana said, 'you leave the organising to me. If the women want to help, you tell them to meet you in the dining room. I'll leave them to you.'

He kissed her and she looked him straight in the eyes. 'I say again,' she warned, 'I'll be like Muriwai if I have to. Kahu, also, if she has to be.'

'You keep Kahu away, e Kui,' Koro Apirana said. 'She's of no use to me.'

With that he had turned to Porourangi and me. As for Kahu, she was staring at the floor, resigned, feeling sorry for herself.

Together, we had all watched the whale with the sacred sign plunging through the sea towards us. The attending herd had fallen back, sending long undulating calls to the unheeding bull whale, which had propelled itself forcefully onto the beach. We had felt the tremor of its landing. As we watched, fearfully, we saw the bull whale heaving itself by muscle contraction even further up the sand. Then, sighing, it had rolled onto its right side and prepared itself for death.

Five or six elderly females had separated from the herd to lie close to the bull whale. They sang to it, attempting to encourage it back to the open sea where the rest of the herd were waiting. But the bull whale remained unmoving.

We had run down to the beach. None of us had been prepared for the physical size of the beast. It seemed to tower over us. A primal psychic force gleamed in its swirling tattoo. Twenty metres long, it brought with it a reminder of our fantastic past.

Then, in the wind and the rain, Koro Apirana had approached the whale. 'Oh, sacred one,' he had called, 'greetings. Have you come to die or to live?' There was no reply to his question. But the whale had raised its giant tail fin, and we had the feeling that this was a decision which had been placed in *our* hands.

It was then that Koro Apirana had asked that the men gather in the meeting house.

Outside there was wind and rain, lightning and thunder. The lightning lit up the beach where the stranded whale was lying. Far out to sea the whale herd waited, confused. Every now and then one of the elderly females would come to comfort the ancient whale and to croon its love for him.

Inside the stomach of the meeting house there was warmth, bewilderment, strength and anticipation, waiting to be soldered into a unity by the words of our chief, Koro Apirana. The sound of the women assembling in the dining room under Nani Flowers' supervision came to us like a song of support. As I shut the door to the meeting house I saw Kahu's face, like a small dolphin, staring out to sea. She was making her mewling noise.

Koro Apirana took us for prayers. His voice rose and fell like the sea. Then he made his greetings to the house, our ancestors, and the tribe gathered inside the house. For a moment he paused, searching for words, then he began to speak.

'Well, boys,' he said, 'there are not many of us. I count twenty-six—'

'Don't forget me, Koro,' a six-year-old interjected.

'Twenty-seven, then,' Koro Apirana smiled, 'so we all have to be one in body, mind, soul and spirit. But first we have to agree on what we must do.' His voice fell silent. 'To explain, I have to talk philosophy and I never went to no university. My university was the school of hard knocks—'

'That's the best school of all,' someone yelled.

'So I have to explain in my own way. Once, our world was one where the Gods talked to our ancestors and man talked with the Gods. Sometimes the Gods gave our ancestors special powers. For instance, our ancestor Paikea' – Koro Apirana gestured to the apex of the house – 'was given power to talk to whales and to command them. In this way, man, beasts and Gods lived in close communion with one another.'

Koro Apirana took a few thoughtful steps back and forward.

'But then,' he continued, 'man assumed a cloak of arrogance and set himself up above the Gods. He even tried to defeat Death, but failed. As he grew in his arrogance he started to drive a wedge through the original oneness of the world. In the passing of Time he divided the world into that half he could believe in and that half he could not believe in. The real and the unreal. The natural and supernatural. The present and the past. The scientific and the fantastic. He put a barrier between both worlds and everything on his side was called rational and everything on the other side was called irrational. Belief in our *Maori* Gods,' he emphasised, 'has often been considered irrational.'

Koro Apirana paused again. He had us in the palms of his hands and was considerate about our ignorance, but I was wondering what he was driving at. Suddenly he gestured to the sea.

'You have all seen the whale,' he said. 'You have all seen the sacred sign tattooed on its head. Is the tattoo there by accident or by design? Why did a whale of its appearance strand itself here and not at Wainui? Does it belong in the real world or the unreal world?'

'The real,' someone called.

'Is it natural or supernatural?'

'It is supernatural,' a second voice said.

Koro Apirana put up his hands to stop the debate. 'No,' he said, 'it is *both*. It is a reminder of the oneness which the world once had. It is the birth cord joining past and present, reality and fantasy. it is both. It is *both*,' he thundered, 'and if we have forgotten the communion then we have ceased to be Maori.'

The wind whistled through his words. 'The whale is a sign,' he began again. 'It has stranded itself here. If we are able to return it to the sea, then that will be proof that the oneness is still with us. If we are not able to return it, then this is because we have become weak. If it lives, we live. If it dies, we die. Not only its salvation but ours is waiting out there.'

Koro Apirana closed his eyes. His voice drifted in the air and hovered, waiting for a decision.

'Shall *we* live? Or shall we die.'

Our answer was an acclamation of pride in our tribe.

Koro Apirana opened his eyes. 'Okay then, boys. Let's go down there and get on with it.'

* * *

Porourangi gave the orders. He told the men that they were to drive every available truck, car, motorbike or tractor down to the bluff overlooking the sea and flood the beach with their headlights. Some of the boys had spotlights which they used when hunting opossums; these, also, were brought to the bluff and trained on the stranded whale. In the light, the whale's tattoo flared like a silver scroll.

Watching from the dining room, Nani Flowers saw Koro Apirana walking around in the rain and got her wild up. She yelled out to one of the boys, '*Hoi*, you take his raincoat to that old paka. Thinks he's Super Maori, ne.'

'What are they doing, Nani?' Kahu asked.

'They're taking all the lights down to the beach,' Nani Flowers answered. 'The whale must be returned to the sea.'

Kahu saw the beams from the headlights of two tractors cutting through the dark. Then she saw her father, Porourangi, and some of the boys running down to the whale with ropes in their hands.

'That's it, boys,' Koro Apirana yelled. 'Now who are the brave ones to go out in the water and tie the ropes around the body of our ancestor? We have to pull him around so that he's facing the sea. Well?'

I saw my friend, Billy, and volunteered on his behalf.

'Gee, thanks, pal,' Billy said.

'I'll take the other rope,' Porourangi offered.

'No,' Koro Apirana said. 'I need you here. Give the rope to your brother, Rawiri.'

Porourangi laughed and threw the rope to me. 'Hey, I'm not your brother,' I said.

He pushed me and Billy out into the sea. The waves were bitingly cold and I was greatly afraid because the whale was so gigantic. As Billy and I struggled to get to the tail all I could think of was that if it rolled I would be squashed just like a banana. The waves lifted us up and down, up and down, up into the dazzle of the lights on the beach and down into the dark sea. Billy must have been as frightened of the whale as I was because he would say, 'Excuse me, koro,' whenever a wave smashed him into the side of the whale, or, 'Oops, sorry koro.'

'Hurry up! Hurry up!' Koro Apirana yelled from the beach. 'We haven't much time. Stop mucking around.'

Billy and I finally managed to get to the tail of the whale. The flukes of the whale were enormous, like huge wings.

'One of us will have to dive underneath,' I suggested to Billy, 'to get the ropes around.'

'Be my guest,' Billy said. He was hanging on for dear life.

There was nothing for it but to do the job myself. I took three deep breaths and dived. The water was churning with sand and small pebbles and I panicked when the whale moved. *Just my luck if it rolled over*, I thought. I sought the surface quickly.

'You're still alive,' Billy shouted in triumph. I passed the two ropes to him. He knotted them firmly and we fought our way back to the beach. The boys gave a big cheer. I heard Billy boasting about how *he* had done all the hard work.

'Now what?' Porourangi asked Koro Apirana.

'We wait,' said Koro Apirana, 'for the incoming tide. The tide will help to float our ancestor and, when he does, we'll use the tractors to pull him around. We will only have the one chance. Then once he's facing the sea we'll all have to get in the water and try to push him out.'

'We could pull him out by boat,' I suggested.

'No, too dangerous,' Koro replied. 'The sea is running too high. The other whales are in the way. No, we wait. And we pray.'

Koro Apirana told Billy and I to get out of our wet clothes. We hopped on my motorbike and went home to change. Naturally, Nani Flowers with her hawk eyes saw us and came ambling over to ask what was happening down on the beach.

'We're waiting for the tide,' I said.

I thought that Nani Flowers would start to growl and protest about not being involved. Instead she simply hugged me and said, 'Tell the old paka to keep warm. I want him to come back to me in one piece.'

Then Kahu was there, flinging herself into my arms. 'Paka? Is Paka all right?'

'Yes, Kahu,' I said.

Suddenly the horns of the cars down on the beach began to sound. The tide was turning. Billy and I rushed to the motorbike and roared back.

'There, there,' Kahu said to Nani Flowers. 'They'll be all right.'

By the time we got back to Koro Apirana the boys were already in action. 'The sea came up so sudden,' Porourangi yelled above the waves. 'Look.'

The whale was already half submerged, spouting in its distress. Three elderly females had managed to come beside him and were trying to nudge him upright before he drowned.

'*Now*,' Porourangi cried. The two tractors coughed into life. The rope took up between them and the whale, and quickly became taut.

With a sudden heave and suck of sand the whale gained its equilibrium. Its eyes opened, and Koro Apirana saw the strength and the wisdom of the ages shining like a sacred flame. The tattoo of the whale too seemed alive with unholy fire.

'Sacred whale,' Koro Apirana said. 'We wish to live. Return to the sea. Return to your kingdom of Tangaroa.'

The tractors began to pull the whale round. By degrees it was lying parallel to the beach. The boys and I put our shoulders to its gigantic bulk and tried to ease it further seaward.

It was then that the ropes snapped. Koro Apirana gave a cry of anguish, burying his face in his hands. Swiftly he turned to me. 'Rawiri, go tell your Nani Flowers it is time for the women to act the men.'

Even before I reached the dining hall Nani Flowers was striding through the rain. The women were following behind her.

'In we go, girls,' Nani Flowers said. 'Kahu, you stay on the beach.'

'But Nani.'

'Stay,' Nani Flowers ordered.

The women ran to join us. Porourangi began to chant encouragement. 'Pull together,' he called. 'Yes, we shall pull together,' we responded. 'Return the whale,' he cried. 'To the ocean,' we answered. We continued chanting as we put our shoulders to the whale, pushing it further seaward and pointing it at the ocean stars.

Out to sea the herd sang its encouragement. The elderly females spouted their joy.

A ripple ran along the back of the whale. A spasm. Our hearts leapt with joy. Suddenly the huge tail rose to stroke at the sky.

The whale moved.

But our joy soon turned to fear. Even as the whale moved, Koro Apirana knew we had lost. For instead of moving out to sea the whale turned on us. The tail crashed into the water causing us to move away, screaming our dread. With a terrifying guttural moan the whale sought deeper where we could not reach it. Then, relentlessly, it turned shoreward again, half-submerging itself in the water, willing its own death.

The wind was rising. The storm was raging. The sea stormed across the sky. We watched, forlorn, from the beach.

'Why?' Kahu asked Koro Apirana.

'Our ancestor wants to die.'

'But why?'

'There is no place for it here in this world. The people who once commanded it are no longer here.' He paused. 'When it dies, we die. I die.'

'*No*, Paka. And if it lives?'

'Then we live also.'

Nani Flowers cradled the old man. She started to lead him away and up to the homestead. The sky forked with lightning. The tribe watched in silence, waiting for the whale to die. The elderly females cushioned it gently in its last resting place. Far out to sea the rest of the herd began the mournful song of farewell for their leader.

Seventeen

Nobody saw her slip away and enter the water. Nobody knew at all until she was half way through the waves. Then the headlights and spotlights from the cars along the beach picked up her white dress and that little head bobbing up and down in the waves. As soon as I saw her, I knew it was Kahu.

'Hey!' I yelled. I pointed through the driving rain. Other spotlights began to catch her. In that white dress and white ribboned pigtails she was like a small puppy, trying to keep its head up. A wave would crash over her but somehow she would appear on the other side, gasping, wide-eyed, and doing what looked like a cross between a dog paddle and a breast stroke.

Instantly I ran through the waves. People said I acted like a maniac. I plunged into the sea.

If the whale lives, we live. These were the only words Kahu could think of. The water was freezing, but not to worry. The waves were huge, but she could do this. The rain was like spears, but she could do this.

Every now and then she had to take a deep breath because sometimes the waves were like dumpers, slamming her down to the sandy bottom, but somehow she bobbed right back up like a cork. The lights from the beach were dazzling her eyes, making it hard to see where she was going. Her neck was hurting with the constant looking up, but *there, there*, was the whale with the tattoo. She dog-paddled purposefully toward it. A wave smashed into her and she swallowed more sea water. She began to cough and tread water. Then she set her face with determination. As she approached the whale, she suddenly remembered what she should do.

'That damn kid,' I swore as I leapt into the surf. For one thing I was no hero and for another I was frightened by the heavy seas. Bathtubs were really the closest I ever like to get to water and at least in a bath the water was hot. This wasn't. It was cold enough to freeze a person. I knew, because I'd only just before been in it.

But I had to admire the kid. She'd always been pretty fearless. Now, here she was, swimming towards the whale. I wondered what on earth she expected to do.

I saw Porourangi running after Koro Apirana and Nani Flowers to bring them back. Then the strangest thing happened. I heard Kahu's high treble voice shouting something to the sea. She was singing to the whale. Telling it to acknowledge her coming.

'Karanga mai, karanga mai, karanga mai.' *Call me*. She raised her head and began to call to the whale.

The wind snatched at her words and flung them with the foam to smash in the wind.

Kahu tried again. 'Oh, sacred ancestor,' she called. 'I am coming to you. I am Kahu. Ko Kahutia Te Rangi ahau.'

The headlights and spotlights were dazzling upon the whale. It may have been the sudden light, or a cross current, but the eye of the whale seemed to flicker. Then the whale appeared to be looking at the young girl swimming.

'Kahu!' I could hear Nani Flowers screaming in the wind.

My boots were dragging me down. I had to stop and reach under to take them off. I lost valuable time, but better that than drown. The boots fell away into the broiling currents.

I looked up. I tried to see where Kahu was. The waves lifted me up and down.

'Kahu, no,' I cried.

She had reached the whale and was hanging onto its jaw. 'Greetings, ancient one,' Kahu said as she clung onto the whale's jaw. 'Greetings.' She patted the whale and looking into its eye, said, 'I have come to you.'

The swell lifted her up and propelled her away from the head of the whale. She choked with the water and tried to dog paddle back to the whale's eye.

'Help me,' she cried. 'Ko Kahutia Te Rangi au. Ko Paikea.'

The whale shuddered at the words.

Ko Paikea?
Ko Kahutia Te Rangi?

By chance, Kahu felt the whale's forward fin. Her fingers tightened quickly around it. She held on for dear life.

And the whale felt a surge of gladness which, as it mounted, became ripples of ecstasy, every increasing. He began to communicate his joy to all parts of his body.

Out beyond the breakwater the herd suddenly became alert. With hope rising, they began to sing their encouragement to their leader.

'Kahu, no,' I cried again.

I panicked and I lost sight of her, and I thought that she had been swept into the whale's huge mouth. I was almost sick thinking about it, but then I remembered that Jonah had lived on in the belly of his whale. So, if necessary, I would just have to go down *this* whale's throat and pull Kahu right out.

The swell lifted me up again. With relief I saw that Kahu was okay. She was hanging onto the whale's forward fin. For a moment I thought my imagination was playing tricks. Earlier, the whale had been lying on its left side. But now it was rolling onto its stomach.

Then I felt afraid that in the rolling Kahu would get squashed. No, she was still hanging onto the fin. I was really frightened though, because in the rolling Kahu had been lifted clear of the water and was now dangling on the side of the whale, like a small white ribbon.

The elderly female whales skirled their happiness through the sea. They listened as the pulsing strength of their leader manifested itself in stronger and stronger whalesong. They crooned tenderness back to him and then throbbed a communication to the younger males to assist their leader. The males arranged themselves in arrow formation to spear through the raging surf.

'Greetings, sacred whale,' Kahu whispered. She was cold and exhausted. She pressed her cheek to the whale's side and kissed the whale. The skin felt like very smooth, slippery rubber.

Without really thinking about it, Kahu began to stroke the whale just behind the fin. *It is my lord, the whale rider.* She felt a tremor in the whale and a rippling under the skin. Suddenly she saw that indentations like footholds and handholds were appearing before her. She tested the footholds and they were firm.

Although the wind was blowing fiercely she stepped away from the sheltering fin and began to climb. As she did so, she caught a sudden glimpse of her Koro Apirana and Nani Flowers clustered with the others on a faraway beach.

I was too late. I saw Kahu climbing the side of the whale. A great wave bore me away from her. I yelled out to her, a despairing cry.

Kahu could climb no further. *It is my lord, Kahutia Te Rangi.* She saw the rippling skin of the whale forming a

103

saddle with fleshy stirrups for her feet and pommels to grasp. She wiped her eyes and smoothed down her hair as she settled herself astride the whale. She heard a cry, like a moan in the wind.

I saw black shapes barrelling through the breakers. Just my luck, I thought. If I don't drown I'll get eaten.

Then I saw that the shapes were smaller whales of the herd, coming to assist their leader.

The searchlights were playing on Kahu astride the whale. She looked so small, so defenceless.

Quietly, Kahu began to weep. She wept because she was frightened. She wept because Paka would die if the whale died. She wept because she was lonely. She wept because she loved her baby sister and her father and Ana. She wept because Nani Flowers wouldn't have anyone to help her in the vegetable garden. She wept because Koro Apirana didn't love her. And she also wept because she didn't know what dying was like.

Then, screwing up her courage, she started to kick the whale as if it was a horse.

'Let us go now,' she shrilled.

The whale began to rise in the water.

'Let us return to the sea,' she cried.

Slowly, the whale began to turn to the open sea. *Yes, my lord.* As it did so, the younger whales came to push their leader into deeper water.

'Let the people live,' she ordered.

Together, the ancient whale and its escort began to swim into the deep ocean.

She was going, our Kahu. She was going into the deep ocean. I could hear her small piping voice in the darkness as she left us.

She was going with the whales into the sea and the rain. She was a small figure in a white dress, kicking at the whale as if it was a horse, her braids swinging in the rain. Then she was gone and we were left behind.

Ko Paikea, ko Paikea.

Eighteen

She was the whale rider. Astride the whale she felt the sting of the surf and rain upon her face. On either side the younger whales were escorting their leader through the surf. They broke through into deeper water.

Her heart was pounding. She saw that now she was surrounded by the whale herd. Every now and then, one of the whales would come to rub alongside the ancient leader. Slowly, the herd made its way to the open sea.

She was Kahutia Te Rangi. She felt a shiver running down the whale and, instinctively, she placed her head against its skin and closed her eyes. The whale descended in a shallow dive and the water was like streaming silk. A few seconds later the whale surfaced, gently spouting.

Her face was wet with sea and tears. The whales were gathering speed, leaving the land behind. She took a quick look and saw headlights far away. Then she felt that same shiver and again placed her head against the whale's skin. This time when the whale dived, it stayed underwater longer. But Kahu had made a discovery. Where her face was pressed the whale had opened up a small breathing chamber.

She was Paikea. In the deepening ocean the fury of the storm was abating. The whale's motions were stronger. As it rose from the sea, its spout was a silver jet in the night sky. Then it dived a third time, and the pressure on her eardrums indicated to the young girl that this was a longer dive than the first two had been. And she knew that the next time would be forever.

She was serene. When the whale broke the surface she made her farewell to sky and earth and sea and land. She called her farewells to her people. She prepared herself as best she could with the little understanding she had. She said goodbye to her Paka, her Nani, her father and mother, her Uncle Rawiri, and prayed for their good health always. She wanted them to live for ever and ever.

The whale's body tensed. The girl felt her feet being locked by strong muscles. The cavity for her face widened. The wind whipped at her hair.

Suddenly the moon came out. Around her the girl could see whales sounding, sounding, sounding. She lowered her face into the whale and closed her eyes. 'I am not afraid to die,' she whispered to herself.

The whale's body arched and then slid into a steep dive. The water hissed and surged over the girl. The huge flukes seemed to stand on the surface of the sea, stroking at the raindrenched sky. Then slowly, they too slid beneath the surface.

She was Kahutia Te Rangi. She was Paikea. She was the whale rider.

Hui e, haumi e, *taiki e*. Let it be done.

The tribe was weeping on the beach. The storm was leaving with Kahu. Nani Flowers' heart was racing and her tears were streaming down her face. She reached into her pockets for a handkerchief. Her fingers curled around a carved stone. She took it out and gave it to Koro Apirana.

'Which of the boys?' he gasped in grief. 'Which of the—'

Nani Flowers was pointing out to sea. Her face was filled with emotion as she cried out to Kahu. The old man understood. He raised his arms as if to claw down the sky upon him.

Epilogue

The Girl from the Sea

Nineteen

In the sunless sea sixty whales were sounding slowly, steeply diving. An ancient bull whale, twenty metres long and bearing a sacred sign, was in the middle of the herd. Flanking him were seven females, half his size, like back-gowned women, shepherding him gently downward.

'Haramai, haramai e koro,' the women sibilantly sang. 'Tomo mai i waenganui i o tatou iwi.' Come old one. Join us, your whole tribe in the sea.

The sea hissed and sparkled with love for the ancient bull whale and, every now and then, the old mother whale would close in on him, gently, to nuzzle him, caress him, and kiss him just to let him know how much he had been missed. But in her heart of hearts she knew that he was badly wounded and near to exhaustion.

From the corner of her eye, the old mother whale noticed a small white shape clasping her husband just behind his tattooed head. She rose to observe the figure and then drifted back beside him.

'Ko wai te tekoteko kei runga?' she sang, her voice musically pulsing. 'Who are you carrying?'

'Ko Paikea, ko Paikea,' the bull whale responded, and the bass notes boomed like an organ through the subterranean cathedral of the sea. I am carrying my lord, Paikea.'

The sea was a giant liquid sky and the whales were descending, plummeting downward like ancient dreams. On either side of the bull whale and his female entourage were warrior whales, te hokowhitu a Tu, swift and sturdy, always alert, a phalanx of fierceness.

'Keep close ranks,' the warrior whales warned. 'Neke neke.'

The leader signalled to some of the warriors to fall back to the rear to close up and tighten the remaining herd of women, men and children.

Meanwhile, the old mother whale was processing the information that the bull whale had given her. 'Ko Paikea? Ko Paikea?' The other women caught flashes of her puzzlement and, curious themselves, rose to look at the motionless rider. One of them nudged the tiny shape and saw a white face like a sleeping dolphin. The female whales hummed their considerations among themselves, trying to figure it all out. Then they shrugged. If the bull whale said it was Paikea, it was Paikea. After all, the bull whale was the boss, the chief.

'Keep close ranks,' the warrior whales whistled reprovingly.

The whales shifted closer together, to support one another, as they fell through the sea.

'Ko Paikea? Ko Paikea?' the old mother whale wondered anxiously. Although she loved her husband, and had done so for many whaleyears, she was not blind to his faults. Over the last few years, for instance, he had become more and more depressed, considering that death was upon him and revisiting the places of his memory. The Valdes Peninsula. Tonga. Galapagos. Tokelau. Easter Island. Rarotonga. Hawaiki, the Island of the Ancients. Antarctica. Now, Whangara, where he had almost been lost to the herd.

Then she knew.

'Halt,' the old mother whale called. In her memory's eye she saw Paikea himself and he was flinging small spears seaward and landward.

Instantly the herd ceased its sounding and became poised in mid-flight between the glassy surface of the sea and the glittering ocean abyss.

The warrior whales glided up to the old mother whale. 'What's the matter?' they trumpeted belligerently. The old mother whale was always calling for a halt.

The old mother whale's heart was pounding. 'I wish to speak,' she said sweetly, 'to my husband.' So saying, she descended gently toward the ancient bull whale.

The sea scintillated with the sweetness of the old mother whale as she hovered near her ancient mate. Illuminated jellyfish exploded silvered starbursts through the dark depths. Far below, a river of phosphorescence lent lambent light to the abyss like a moonlit tide. The ocean was alive with noises: dolphin chatter, krill hiss, squid thresh, shark swirl, shrimp click, and, ever present, the strong swelling chords of the sea's constant rise and fall.

'E koro,' the old mother whale began in a three-tone sequence drenched with love. 'My dear lord,' she continued, adding a string of harmonics. 'My man,' she breathed with slyness, threading her words with sensuous major arpeggios, 'the rider that you carry isn't Paikea.'

The other female whales edged away carefully but they secretly admired the courage of the old mother whale in questioning the identity of the whale rider.

'Yes, it is Paikea,' the bull whale said, insistent, 'it's Paikea.'

The old mother whale cast her eyes downward, hoping that the bull whale would take this as a sign of feminine submission, but she knew in fact what she was up to.

'No, no, my lord,' she belled sweetly.

The female whales gasped at the old mother whale's stubbornness. The warrior whales waited for the word from their leader to teach her a lesson.

The bull whale responded in a testy manner. 'Of course it is! When my lord mounted me, he said his name was Kahutia Te Rangi.' Surely the old mother whale should know this was another name for Paikea. 'Ko Kahutia Te Rangi ko Paikea.'

The old mother whale allowed herself to drift just below her husband.

'Perhaps, perhaps,' she trilled in soprano tones of innocent guile.

The other female whales now decided to give her a wide berth.

The old mother whale saw the warrior whales preparing to give her a sharp nip in the behind. She moved quickly toward the ancient bull whale and let a fin accidentally on purpose caress the place of his deepest pleasure. 'But,' she told him, 'I can see the rider and it's not who you think it is.' She gave her head two shakes to emphasise that when she had looked at the rider it didn't look like Paikea at all. Instead, the rider looked like a human girl. 'Perhaps it's a descendant of your lord?' she asked modestly. 'Think back, husband.' Her song inflected the questions with graceful ornamentation.

The other female whales nodded to each other. She was clever all right, the old mother whale. By asking questions she was enabling their leader to come to the decision she had already reached. No wonder she was the queen and they were the ladies in waiting.

The ancient bull whale waved the warrior whales away; he was getting irritated with them and their fancy drills.

'Think back?' he repeated to himself. And through the mists of time he saw his master, Paikea, flinging wooden spears into the sky. Some in midflight became birds. And others on reaching the sea turned into eels. And he, Paikea himself, was a spear populating the land and sea so that it was no longer barren.

The ancient bull whale began to assess the weight of the rider. It was light all right, and the legs were shorter than he remembered, and—

'Yes,' the old mother whale crooned, agreeing with the decision he hadn't yet made. 'This is the last spear, the one which was to flower in the future.' She let the words sink in. She wanted to make sure that the bull whale really understood that the rider was Paikea's descendant and, if it was not returned to the surface and taken back to the land, then it would not fulfil its tasks. 'It is the seed of Paikea,' she said, 'and we must return it to the land.' In her voice was ageless music.

The ancient bull whale swayed in the silken tides of the stirring sea. Though tired, he sensed the truth in his consort's words. For he remembered that Paikea had hesitated before throwing the last of his wooden spears and, when he did this, he had said, 'Let this one be planted in the years to come when the people are troubled and it is most needed.' And the spear, soaring through the sky, came to rest in the earth where the afterbirth of a female child would be placed.

And as he remembered, the bull whale began to lose his nostalgia for the past and to put his thoughts to the present and the future. Surely, in the tidal wave of Fate, there must have been a reason for his living so long. It could not have been coincidence that he should return to Whangara and be ridden by a descendant of his beloved golden master. Perhaps his fate and that of the rider on top of him were inextricably intertwined? Ah yes, for nothing would have been left to chance.

As they waited for the ancient bull whale's judgment, the herd began to add the colour of their opinion. The female whales chattered that they knew all along the old mother whale was right, and the warrior whales, seeing the way things were going, agreed.

The ancient bull whale gave a swift gesture.

'We must return to the surface,' he commanded, readying himself for a quick ascent. 'We must return this new rider back to Whangara. Do we all agree?'

The herd sang a song of agreement to their ancient leader's decision.

'Yes, yes, yes,' they chorused in a song of benign tenderness. 'Ae. Ae. Ae.'

Slowly, the phalanx of whales began their graceful procession to the surface of the sea, broadcasting their orchestral affirmation to the universe.

Hui e, haumi e, taiki e.

Let it be done.

Twenty

After Kahu's departure, Nani Flowers collapsed. She was taken to the hospital where, five days later, her eyelids flickered open. She saw Koro Apirana sitting next to the bed. Me and the boys were also there.

Nani Flowers shook herself awake. The nurse and Koro Apirana helped her to sit up. Once she had gotten comfortable she closed her eyes a second time. Then she peeked out of one eye and sighed.

'Hmm,' she said sarcastically. 'If you lot are still here that must mean I haven't gone to Heaven.'

But we didn't mind her sarcasm because we were used to her being an old grump. Koro Apirana looked at her lovingly.

'You have to lose some weight, Putiputi,' he said to her. 'Your heart is too weak. I don't know what I would have done if the both of you—'

Nani Flowers suddenly remembered. 'What has happened to Kahu—'

Koro Apirana quietened her quickly. 'No, no, Flowers,' he said. 'She's all right. She's all right.' He told Nani Flowers what had happened.

Three days after the sacred whale and its accompanying herd had gone, and after Kahu had been given up for dead, she had been found unconscious, floating in a nest of dark lustrous kelp in the middle of the ocean. How she got there nobody knew, but when she was found the dolphins that were guarding her sped away with happy somersaults and leaps into the air.

Kahu had been rushed to the hospital. Her breathing had stopped, started, stopped and then started again. She was now off the respirator but she was still in a coma. The doctors did not know whether she would regain consciousness.

'Where is she? Where's my Kahu?' Nani Flowers cried.

'She's here with you,' Koro Apirana said. 'Right here in this same hospital. Me and the tribe have been looking over you both, waiting for you to come back to us. You two have been each other's strength.'

Koro Apirana gestured to the other bed in the room. The boys separated and, through the gap, Nani Flowers saw Kahu, her face waxed and still.

The tears streamed down Nani Flowers' cheeks.

'Push my bed over to her bed,' Nani said. 'I'm too far away from her. I want to hold her and talk to her.'

The boys huffed and puffed with pretended exertion.

'Now all of you Big Ears can wait outside the door,' Nani said. 'Just leave me and your Koro here alone with our Kahu.'

She was like a little doll. Her eyes were closed and her eyelashes looked very long against her pallid skin. White ribbons had been used to tie her hair. There was no colour in her cheeks, and she seemed not to be breathing at all.

The bedcovers had been pulled right up to Kahu's chin, but her arms were on top of the covers. She was wearing warm flannel pyjamas, and the pyjama top was buttoned up to her neck.

The minutes passed. Koro Apirana and Nani Flowers looked at each other, and their hearts ached.

'You know, dear,' Koro Apirana said. 'I blame myself for this. It's all my fault.'

'Yeah, it sure is,' Nani Flowers wept.

'I should have known she was the one,' Koro Apirana

said. 'Ever since that time when she was a baby and bit my toe.'

'Boy, if only she had real teeth,' Nani Flowers agreed.

'And all those times I ordered her away from the meeting house, I should have known.'

'You were deaf, dumb, blind *and* stubborn.'

The window to the room was half open. The sunlight shone through the billowing curtains. Nani Flowers noticed that the door was slowly inching open and that the nosey visitors were looking in. Talk about no privacy, with them out there with their eyes all red and the tears coming out.

'You never even helped with Kahu's birth cord,' Nani Flowers sobbed.

'You're right, dear, I've been no good.'

'Always telling Kahu she's no use because she's a girl. Always growling at her. Growl, growl, growl.'

'And I never knew,' Koro Apirana said, 'until you showed me the stone.'

'I should have cracked you over the head with it, you old paka.'

Dappled shadows chased each other across the white walls. On the window sill were vases of flowers in glorious profusion.

Koro Apirana suddenly got up from his chair. His face was filled with the understanding of how rotten he had been.

'You should divorce me,' he said to Nani Flowers. 'You should go and marry old Waari over the hill.'

'Yeah, I should, too,' Nani Flowers said. 'He knows how to treat a woman. He wouldn't trample on my Muriwai blood as much as you have.'

'You're right, dear, you're right.'

'I'm always right, you old paka, and—'

Suddenly Kahu gave a long sigh. Her eyebrows began to knit as if she was thinking of something.

'You two are always arguing,' she breathed.

* * *

The whales were rising from the sea. Their skins were lucent and their profiles were gilded with the moon's splendour. Rising, rising.

'Does the rider still live?' the ancient bull whale asked. He was concerned that the rider was okay, still breathing.

'Yes,' the old mother whale nodded. She had been singing gently to the whale rider, telling her not to be afraid.

'Very well,' the ancient bull whale said. 'Then let everyone live, and let the partnership between land and sea, whales and all humankind, also remain.'

And the whale herd sang their gladness that the tribe would also live because they knew that the girl would need to be carefully taught before she could claim the place for her people in the world.

The whales breached the surface and the thunderous spray was like silver fountains in the moonlight.

Twenty-one

Nani Flowers gave an anguished sob and reached out to hold Kahu tightly. Koro Apirana tottered to the bedside and looked down at the sleeping girl. He began to say a prayer, and he asked the Gods to forgive him. He saw Kahu stir.

Oh, *yes*, grandchild. Rise up from the depths of your long sleep. Return to the people and take your rightful place among them.

Kahu drew another breath. She opened her eyes. 'Is it time to wake up now?' she asked.

Nani Flowers began to blubber. Koro Apirana's heart skipped a beat. 'Yes. It is time to return.'

'They told me not to wake until you were both here,' Kahu said gravely.

'Who are you talking about?' Koro Apirana asked.

'The whales,' she said. Then she smiled, 'You two sounded just like the old mother whale and the bull whale arguing.'

Nani Flowers looked up at Koro Apirana. 'We don't argue,' she said, '*He* argues and *I* win.'

'Your Muriwai blood,' Koro Apirana said. 'Always too strong for me.'

Kahu giggled. She paused. Then her eyes brimmed with sadness. In a small voice she said, 'I fell off.'

'What?'

'I fell off the whale. If I was a boy I would have held on tight. I'm sorry, Paka, I'm not a boy.'

The old man cradled Kahu in his arms, partly because of emotion and partly because he didn't want those big ears out there to hear their big chief crying.

'You're the best grandchild in the whole wide world,' he said. 'Boy or girl, it doesn't matter.'

'Really, Paka?' Kahu gasped. She hugged him tightly and pressed her face against him. 'Oh, thank you, Paka. You're the best granddad in the whole wide world.'

'I love you,' Koro Apirana said.

'Me too,' Nani Flowers added.

'And don't forget about us,' said the rest of the tribe as they crowded into the room.

Suddenly, in the joyous melee, Kahu raised a finger to her lips: *Sssshh*.

The ancient bull whale breached the surface, leaping high into the moonlit sky. The sacred sign, the tattoo, was agleam like liquid silver. The bull whale flexed his muscles, releasing Kahu, and she felt herself tumbling along his back, tumbling, tumbling, tumbling. All around her the whales were leaping, and the air was filled with diamond spray.

'Can't you hear them?' Kahu asked.

She fell into the sea. The thunder of the whales departing was loud in her ears. She opened her eyes and looked downward. Through the foaming water she could see huge tail fins waving farewell.

Then from the backwash of Time came the voice of the old mother whale. 'Child, your people await you. Return to the Kingdom of Tane and fulfil your destiny.' And suddenly the sea was drenched again with a glorious echoing music from the dark shapes sounding.

Kahu looked at Koro Apirana, her eyes shining.

'Oh, *Paka*, can't you hear them? I've been listening to them for ages now. Oh, *Paka*, and the whales are still singing,' she said.

Haumi e, hui e, *taiki e*.

Let it be done.

The best in classic and

Jane Austen

Elizabeth Laird

Beverley Naidoo   Roddy Doyle

Robert Swindells

George Orwell

Charles Dickens

Charlotte Brontë

Jan Mark

Anne Fine

Anthony Horowitz